"Wounds and voices from our past often become the loudest in our heads, yielding shame, silence and suffering. These burdens are wearisome. They prevent us from loving ourselves and others, and keep us from living our best lives. Daphne tells her story and comes along side you with wisdom, grit and grace. *What's YOUR Scarlet Letter* will help you journey from lies to truth, reclaim what was taken from you, and embrace the wonder of you!"

—Susie Miller, MA, MDiv, Speaker | Catalyst |
Author of Listen, Learn, Love: How to Dramatically
Improve Your Relationships in 30 Days or Less!

"Lies. Lies. Lies. They trap us well beneath our potential. Author, Daphne Smith, unlocks the secret to emotional healing by demonstrating in word and deed the faith-filled power of releasing truth and exposing evil. Daphne's words speak abundant life to all who know there is more light within them to discover."

—Dr. Harold Arnold, Host of *The Leading You Home Podcast*
and Author of *Second Shift: How to Grow Your Part-time
Passion to Full-Time Influence*

"You are made for more. Hiding because of hurt and shame robs us of our voice. *What's YOUR Scarlet Letter* recognizes our pain and provides a way to our full potential in freedom."

—Jevonnah "Lady J" Ellison, Certified Master Coach
Founder, The Leading Ladies Mastermind jevonnah.com

"What's YOUR Scarlet Letter brings us from pain and shame to healing and wholeness. Clinging to hope is the light in darkness. There is no need to live with the pain of abuse, divorce, rejection or other hurts we encounter in life."

—Julie Gorman, co-owner of Gorman leadership group, and co-author of Married for a Purpose and Two are Better Then One

"What's holding you back? Your Scarlet Letter will help you discover the hidden lies within. God's love and truth can set you free. Go for it!"

—Betty Southard- Speaker, Author, Spiritual Director, bettysouthard.com

"Secrets keep us imprisoned. Daphne helps you plan an escape. Admitting we have hurts is the first step to breaking free from the lies we've come to believe as truth. Knowing Daphne's vibrant character and a little of her emergence from behind the veil, I couldn't wait to read and learn from her life lessons."

—Gill Scott, Author and Facilitator of Disentangled Genius

"Life doesn't always go as planned. Hurts happen and can cause us to question our future. *What's YOUR Scarlet Letter* reminds of us healing through hope."

—Melissa J. Nixon, Author of The Courageous Life, Speaker, and Career and Business Coach for Women of Faith

# What's YOUR Scarlet Letter

### Recognize Your Hurts
### Release Your Shame
### Reclaim Your Voice

# What's YOUR Scarlet Letter

### Recognize Your Hurts
### Release Your Shame
### Reclaim Your Voice

DAPHNE V. SMITH

**AUTHOR ACADEMY** elite

Printed in the United States of America

Published by Author Academy Elite
P.O. Box 43, Powell, OH 43035

www.AuthorAcademyElite.com

Paperback ISBN: 978-1-64085-238-9
Hardcover ISBN: 978-1-64085-239-6

Library of Congress Control Number: 2018934730

To my baby girl, Erica.
From the moment you were born, I wanted to be the best mom possible for you by loving and leading you through example. At times and in part, that meant dealing with my own demons.

I am over the moon proud of you and for you.
You are a woman of strength, love, grace, loyalty, and courage.
Thank you for helping and inspiring me to become one as well.

# CONTENTS

Foreword by Kary Oberbrunner..................xiii

Preface: Everyone's Been Hurt.............. xv

**Part 1**  **Recognize Your Hurt**..................1

He Loves Me, He Loves Me Not .............3

Other Childhood Games........................11

The Big "D" and Other Letters.................25

Healing Your Hurt ...............................39

**Part 2**  **Release Your Shame** ............. 45

Shame Shame Go Away ........................47

It Wasn't Your Fault...............................51

Exposing the Lies..................................59

What If It Only Happened Once?...........65

No Excuse for Abuse .............................73

Surrender Your Shame...........................81

**Part 3**  **Reclaim Your Voice** ............. 89

It's Okay to Tell "Secrets" .......................91

Shatter the Stronghold ..........................95

Take Back What was Taken....................99

Victory In Your Voice............................105

Final Thoughts........................................111

Appendix..............................................117

Additional Resources...........................119

Suggested Books ..................................121

About the Author..................................123

Acknowledgements ..............................125

Opportunities for Connection ............127

All alone I have cried
Silent tears full of pride
In a world made of steel
Made of stone

Irene Cara, Flashdance....What a Feeling

# FOREWORD

On February 22, 2014, I met Daphne V. Smith at a Starbucks in Florida. A mutual friend of ours told me I needed to talk to her. Evidently, she thought I could help her. In Daphne's own words at that time in her life she was a "hot mess."

I didn't think so.

Instead, I saw a woman on fire...a kindred spirit. Sure, Daphne may have been in pain that day, but we all are at some time. The difference with Daphne was that she was honest enough to admit it. And that's why she experienced dramatic transformation shortly after.

Fast-forward to today and I don't even recognize her. Instead, she is blazing! A word I use to describe her is: fearless. She rolls up her sleeves and dives straight into whatever obstacles dare to oppose her.

I saw this tendency a couple years ago—that's why I invited her to join our team and take over one of the most important roles in our business. She has been a true master at everything she sets her mind to do, out-performing my expectations on a regular basis.

I've been blessed to meet her husband David, too. Together they're a power couple, but it wasn't always so. And this is the exactly why you need to read this book—*What's Your Scarlet Letter?*

This is the story of every single one of us. Unworthy and in need of God's grace, regrettably only some of us are brave enough to admit our brokenness. But within that admission we discover true hope and healing.

Sure, Daphne's story will inspire you. Yet, more than that it will empower you to experience deeper levels of freedom in your own journey. Brace yourself. This is your moment to recognize your hurts, release your shame, and reclaim your voice.

Kary Oberbrunner

CEO of Redeem the Day and Igniting Souls
Author of *Elixir Project, Day Job to Dream Job, The Deeper Path,* and *Your Secret Name*

# EVERYONE'S BEEN HURT

In Nathaniel Hawthorne's classic novel, The Scarlet Letter, one of the main characters (dare I label her a heroine?) lives a life of public shame and ridicule due to a choice she made. She kept the origin of that a choice a secret; bearing its pain for decades. Although, if you are familiar with the story, you might recall there was a portion of her secret she couldn't keep hidden after 9 months.

Hester, the woman to whom I am referring, was hurt and bore shame by choices she made.

However, that's not everyone's story. Some of us wear our pain visibly, as a scarlet letter if you will. While others hide behind a mask. Either method is an attempt to cover either their self-inflicted or others-induced pain.

Hurt. It's the one emotion every human has in common and experiences in their lifetime.

There is absolutely not one single person who has never been hurt. The types of hurt we encounter can range from a skinned knee to a scarred soul. What we do with that hurt, how we allow that pain to affect us, truly impacts our lives.

Was it a typical life happening like a boo-boo or disappointment? You know, the type of occurrence experienced in an average "normal" childhood.

Perhaps, it was more invasive and intense such as abuse, abortion, divorce, infidelity and or body image to mention only a few.

If it was the latter types of pain, how we process our experience and the feelings associated with it will have a direct correlation to our healing. Do we work through the pain and allow the wounds to heal? Or do we bury them and try to ignore the offenses?

Sometimes things happen to us that hurt as the result of another's actions, sometimes our own actions, and sometimes it may simply appear to be random.

How, in fact, do we actually define hurt? What is painful to one person could simply bounce off and practically go unnoticed by another. Hurt can be defined as something that causes mental or physical pain; something that is detrimental. Synonyms include distress, harm, ruin, devastation, injury, and abuse.

I think the range of descriptions adds to the complexity and challenge in understanding our own hurt as well as that of another.

**What's YOUR Scarlet Letter** is a guide to recognize your hurt, release your shame, and reclaim your voice. It's a journey of letting go in order to experience healing, transformation, and freedom.

> "Owning our story can be hard but not nearly as difficult as spending our lives running from it. Embracing our vulnerabilities is risky but not nearly as dangerous as giving up on love and belonging and joy - the experiences that make us the most vulnerable. Only when we are brave enough to explore the darkness will we discover the infinite power of our light."

—Brene Brown from The Gifts of Imperfection

I believe in being prepared for a journey. Call it my childhood experiences with camping or my grown up issues with control. Either way, I like to know what to expect.

I've created a FREE resource for you as you begin this journey. It's called 3 Things to Expect with Change. Simply visit DaphneVSmith.com/3Things.

We can't be prepared for everything we experience in life. We can start with awareness and there's a bit of peace and comfort that go along with it.

It's time to live free, secure, and empowered!

With encouragement and belief!
Daphne

# RECOGNIZE YOUR HURT

*"Don't hold to anger, hurt or pain.*
*They steal your energy and keep you from love."*
*– Leo Buscaglia*

# HE LOVES ME, HE LOVES ME NOT

I remember the nonsensical game of plucking flower petals one at a time and reciting, "He loves me, he loves me not." Whichever petal was the last to be removed was my romantic fate with a dreamy-eyed prince or current star crush. It was a fun way to fantasize about love.

I *wish* real love were that innocent and easy to determine. But I grew up with a skewed understanding of love and it took decades to decipher what real love looks like, acts like, and sounds like coming from the opposite sex.

As children, we often have adult or sometimes young adult caregivers. Part of their duty is to teach us life lessons and impress upon us the difference between right and wrong. "Don't touch the hot stove." "Look both ways before crossing the street." "Share your toys."

They can also be responsible to protect and provide for us. Simple tasks like turning on the light when we're scared of the dark and checking for monsters under the bed. Caring gestures like serving you chicken noodle soup when you're under the weather. These are common practices learned from and through a healthy, loving provider.

But what if…what if that caregiver betrays their responsibility to you and violates your very being?

*The smells of cabbage cooking and the warmth radiating from the stovetop brought a certain type of comfort as it meant I was in a safe place; I was away from him. I believe his wife actually tried to protect me or at least minimize my exposure. I think that's why I spent so much time sitting at the laminate topped kitchen table. She was able to keep me close by and within eye sight.*

*However, at the time, sitting hour after hour felt like punishment instead of safety. I assume this is also where my food addiction began. Food literally represented comfort. While I wasn't necessarily consuming the food, being around it represented a certain type of protection and comfort. In fact, the smell of cooked cabbage which seemed to be their daily diet is today more offensive than appetizing. It often serves as a trigger.*

*I still have vivid memories of my time spent in the home of my first perpetrator. I can see the table pressed against the wall and the TV on the shelf above. I used to sit there and play "Office;" pretending I was the boss while The Price is Right, That Girl, and Get Smart played in the background.*

*It served as the beginning of my need to escape reality.*

*I may never fully remember the extent of my assault. And honestly, I'm okay with that. What I do remember is enough to let me know something happened. Something inappropriate involving his hand, my personal parts and a blue blanket trimmed in satin. I remember their dark hallway, the bathroom, a closet in the living room, pictures of their daughter on the wall. Random bits and pieces forming an incomplete puzzle.*

*I do remember being warned or perhaps coerced not to tell. As the oldest of three girls all under the same watch of this couple, I felt the responsibility to keep the peace. To literally keep my mouth shut. In fact, being quiet as to not wake the baby was part of keeping the secret and being a good girl. And if I was a good girl, maybe he wouldn't hurt my sisters as well.*

I thought fatherly, or in this case grandfatherly, figures were supposed to hug and love on me. It meant they cared and I had their attention. That felt normal. In fact, I grew up around a lot of men who did treat me well. My dad, my grandfather, my uncle, each and everyone loved and adored me in appropriate ways. However, the type of attention I got from *him* was and is never okay under any circumstances. It wasn't love. It wasn't caring for me. It was feeding his own sick need.

Several years after leaving the couple's care, I learned my offender had suffered a heart attack. My immediate thought after hearing the news was, "So, who cares." Now, even for a typical apathetic teenager, that's a bit harsh. It even struck me at the time as being a bit cold.

Decades later when I recalled the suppressed memories, they shocked me like a lightning bolt.

Out of the blue, while I was sitting in my sunroom during my morning devotion time, the feelings began to flood. I can still picture my spot on the couch. Suddenly images flashed in my mind. My body experienced a visceral reaction like a giant heat wave washing over and through me.

I knew right at that moment I had a choice. Dig deep to reveal the cause or bury it. I chose to dig and extract. I was tired of denying that nagging feeling and distant memory that I held at bay and silenced out of fear each time it tried to rear its ugly head.

Once I had the lightning bolt recollection, I understood my response to the earlier heart attack news. This man had hurt me. Why would I care if he had experienced any pain?

Sexual assault, abuse, molestation. Whatever it was, it didn't feel right. At the time it happened, I didn't know how to label it or who to tell, if anybody.

Not long after my recovered memory, I shared my story with my mom. Before I could even tell her who it was, she guessed. She shared with me that one day when she came to pick up my sisters and me all those years ago, this same man tried to put his hand up her shirt. If only she'd known that was a signal.

Please understand, I harbor no blame toward my mom. Back in the early 70s this was not something anyone spoke about in any venue. We didn't even have the concept of stranger danger at the time. It was a simpler time where trust was assumed and freely given. A seven year old back then was not equipped to say no. I was raised to use my manners, not to talk back, do as I was told, and respect my elders. Be seen and not heard.

That childhood encounter went on to influence my choices during my teenage and young adult years, especially my understanding of what was appropriate in a healthy relationship; even how I viewed love. Too often I sought acceptance and acknowledgement in unhealthy ways. Acts that didn't connect me at a heart and soul level to others. After a slew of poor choices and through lots of healing, I learned sex is not love. Those encounters ultimately scarred my soul and distorted my perception of my worth and value.

*I vividly recall an incident as a teenager in my own home, my own room to be exact.*

*I had been allowed to take a boy back there. Even though my mom instructed the door remain open, my bedroom was at the far end of the hall and I was a rebellious teenager; so I quietly closed the door.*

*I can still picture the scene. It's as though I am hovering over it having an out of body experience. I was still so naive, so scared.*

*My perpetrator was an upper classmate, a well-known star athlete at our high school. While we were kissing, he took my hand and guided it toward his zipper. He was bigger and stronger than me. He forced me to touch him and maintain contact as he ejaculated. He felt relief. I felt violated and dirty. I felt shame and betrayal; used, yet again. I thought this boy really liked me.*

*My head and gut were in conflict from the beginning. I experienced both the initial typical thrill of disobeying a parent coupled with having a boy in my room. I knew I was already breaking the rules by closing my door.*

*The fear of being punished for disobeying was far greater than the atrocity of another assault. If I had screamed out, what would have happened? How would my mother have reacted? Would I be the one in trouble? Instead, I chose to remain silent.*

I lived with that secret for years. How could I tell anyone? Hadn't I "asked for it" by inviting him into my room? My thoughts and emotions blurred.

I couldn't separate right from wrong because I didn't know at the time there was a clear line. My instincts and gut development had already been interrupted earlier in life. This confusion opened me up for other violations along the way.

I too often gave myself away in hopes of being treasured.

I thought they cared for me. I thought, perhaps, they loved me. After all, they paid attention to me and didn't yell at me or hit me. They took what they wanted and came back for more, most of the time. While I knew what was happening didn't feel "right," I didn't know I could say no or make it stop.

What kind of girl did this make me? Did my occasional stimulation mean I liked it? I was confused with no one and nowhere to turn. So I used the only coping mechanisms I knew at the time - I clammed-up and closed-off. If I stopped feeling, I couldn't be hurt anymore. Instead,

I stuffed my feelings with food to protect and comfort myself. I finally had something I knew I had control over.

Affection, abuse, sex, love. How does one learn the difference when one's basic model is so wrong? The first step is to seek knowledge. When we educate ourselves and those in our care, we become empowered. Empowerment can lead to equipping. With new equipment, we can engage differently.

"Sexual assault can be a violent, unexpected, traumatic and sometimes life threatening event or series of events. Sexual assault is ANY unwanted sexual act or behavior which is threatening, violent, forced or coercive and to which a person has not given consent or was not able to give consent.

Sexual abuse is when someone in a position of power or authority takes advantage of a person's trust and respect to involve them in sexual activity. It can involve any of the examples above." [*1]

Have you ever heard of a woman named Gomer? She lived thousands of years ago and had also been abused sexually. Even after she was "rescued by a prince," there were times she fell back into the ways which were familiar to her. No matter how much pain we experience, sadly, there is a certain type of comfort that comes from the known.

I, too, tried to out-run and deny my past; to cover up my sins and shame.

However, early in my life a seed of hope had been buried deep inside me. Somewhere far below the surface and suffering, I knew I had value. My maternal grandmother even had a nickname for me. She called me- special angel.

When I decided to stop hiding and running, I was able to accept unconditional, perfect love. The kind of love offered to each and every one of us. This love comes from a selfless sacrifice made on my behalf through my Savior.

Once I began to understand my value regardless of my past, I was able to recognize all of my hurts; the choices I made and the choices others made for me. I now know there is no perfect love outside of Jesus Christ.

I realized I needed to stop seeking affection and love from fellow fallen people. My value is not determined by another's treatment of me. It's not determined, by the number of petals on a flower.

# OTHER CHILDHOOD GAMES

## Sticks and Stones May Break My Bones...

Let's finish it together, "Sticks and stones may break my bones but words will never harm me."

This apparently sassy childhood comeback is, in truth, a big fat lie! Words hurt. From The Bible to Shakespeare there are references to the power of the tongue. Images of a two-edged sword are related to the weapon known as words.

A two-edged sword, picture it. A knife with serrated blades on both sides. I've read that a sword of this sharpness can cut through bone! It's no wonder then, when cruel words come out of someone's mouth, they literally cut through us and can wound our soul.

Bitch. Fat ass. Lazy. Stupid. I wish you were never born. Loser. You were a mistake. I never really loved you.

Can you relate to any of those words or phrases? Did you have a visceral reaction when you read them? If you close your eyes, can you almost hear the words and envision the person speaking them?

If so, you understand verbal abuse. This type of abuse or assault causes damage that is never seen by the naked eye and yet it still leaves a scar. It cuts deep. Each time the words echo in our mind, we reopen and irritate the wound. (That is, until we replace those words and images with truth, which we will discuss and implement later in this book.)

First, let me back-up a bit. There is a definite and distinct difference between verbal abuse and teasing. Light-hearted teasing usually ends in a chuckle by both the one saying the words and the one to whom the words are directed. They can even result in a pat on the back or a hug. An old-fashioned "ribbing" can actually bond people together. While teasing is not nice, and often immature, it can be carried to an extreme, crossing into abuse.

Another term for verbal abuse is verbal bullying. This form of abuse can be described as a negative, defining statement spoken either to the victim or about the victim. Verbal abuse creates wedges and distance between the one voicing the words and the one to whom they are directed.

Perhaps it was a random comment said out of the blue. It may have been muttered under their breath, barely audible. Other times it is screamed repeatedly in privacy, assumedly out of earshot from others; making the wounds deeper because of the isolation of the attack.

Sometimes, it is blurted out in a front of a crowd, maybe just once, yet in a way that causes an immediate impact because of the embarrassment of a public degrading. Regardless of the delivery, once the words are spoken, a "do over" or "take back" can't undo or remove the betrayal. We can't un-hear what's been said.

*I recall the end of a first date with a fellow co-worker. We'll call him Kirk. He drove me home after going out to dinner one night. As we stood outside his car to say goodbye, he whispered these words into my ear, "If I said you had a beautiful body, would you hold it against me?"*

*I naively replied, "No." I could tell by the look on his face my reply was very confusing to him.*

*I thought he meant would I be offended if he said I had a beautiful body. For those who know country music, they understand that what he whispered were song lyrics. But I wasn't familiar with the song. He had to explain to me what he meant. I was also under the age of 18 at the time and he was in his mid-20s.*

That incident, while inappropriate due to the age difference and the fact we worked together, might have been innocent enough. I believe he was flirting with me in the hopes of more than a goodnight kiss. I don't personally consider it verbal abuse.

What about a passive aggressive verbal attack? These are extremely confusing. Was it a sincere compliment intended to flatter? Was it flirtation? Was it an inappropriate solicitation?

The off-handed compliment and stare down the front of my dress from my coworker - was it a compliment that

I was being noticed or was it clearly sexual harassment? I hadn't shown any interest, requested or solicited any attention from him.

**And if we don't talk about it, then it was harmless. Right? WRONG!**

At the time it happened, in the early 80's, it sadly was common corporate culture. Even though he worked in the mailroom and I had a higher position in the company, I never said a word to anyone. Unfortunately, there are still situations taking place like this even today. And if we don't talk about it, then it was harmless. Right? WRONG!

There are, however, definitive differences between a compliment, a flirtation, and a proposition.

A compliment builds the receiver up. It honors them, pointing out a positive character trait or attribute.

Flirting is sexual teasing. There are no intentions of anything developing. It's meant for amusement. Often the recipient initially feels admired. Shortly after the flirtation has ended, or perhaps during, the feeling can change from admiration to guilt, shame or embarrassment. Age difference is also a significant factor in these situations.

A proposition is explicitly sexual in nature. They are the most obvious and potentially offensive. In certain situations a couple may use this type of communication as foreplay. When this is the case, it is consensual. When it is out of the blue and unsolicited, that's a different situation.

Once the soul-scarring from verbal abuse has taken place, then what? How do we recover? A broken arm, a bruise, those type of wounds have a natural healing time and course. The internal can be harder to heal.

Humiliation is when one feels disgraced, belittled, or made to look foolish. Words can evoke such emotions. It's not always a physical action responsible for creating abuse or assault.

In total honesty and full transparency, some of my verbal abuse was self-inflicted.

Yes, we can cause harm to our own souls. Anytime we make a mistake and call ourselves an idiot or berate ourselves, we are self-injuring. Years ago when I was at an unhealthy weight and displeased with my appearance, I used to refer to myself as cow woman. We don't always need someone else to say hurtful things. We can cause damage ourselves.

What worked for me was to acknowledge the reality of the hurt. Putting on a brave front and pretending the words hadn't offended was only adding insult to my injury. Being honest with myself without judgement, allowed me to begin to let go.

Some may say, "Develop a thick skin;" or "Stop being so sensitive." Those phrases alone show a lack of awareness about the power of words. Remember, words can be used as a weapon. No one else has permission to tell us how to feel when we've been hurt by a verbal assault, even if it was self-inflicted.

Words can hurt as much or more than sticks and stones.

## Hide and Go Seek

Did you ever play this popular childhood game growing up? The thrill of the hunt, the cunning of hiding with hopes of not being discovered. But what if...what if you're never sought? What if you hid and no one came looking for you? If that ever happened to you, then you understand emotional abuse.

One definition of emotional abuse is: "any act including confinement, isolation, verbal assault, humiliation, intimidation, infantilization, or any other treatment which may diminish the sense of identity, dignity, and self-worth."[1]

Emotional abuse is also known as *psychological abuse* or as "chronic verbal aggression" by researchers. People who suffer from emotional abuse tend to have very low self-esteem, show personality changes (such as becoming withdrawn) and may even become depressed, anxious or suicidal.- Natasha Tracy as published on Healthy Place for your mental health

Passive/aggressive behavior is considered covert abuse.

In some countries emotional abuse is defined. The following examples of emotional abuse are given by Justice Canada:

- Threats of violence or abandonment
- Intentionally frightening
- Making an individual fear that they will not receive the food or care they need
- Lying
- Failing to check allegations of abuse against them
- Making derogative or slanderous statements

about an individual to others
- Socially isolating an individual, failing to let them have visitors
- Withholding important information
- Demeaning an individual because of the language they speak
- Intentionally misinterpreting traditional practices
- Repeatedly raising the issue of death
- Telling an individual that they are too much trouble
- Ignoring or excessively criticizing
- Being over-familiar and disrespectful

Unreasonably ordering an individual around; treating an individual like a servant or child[*2]

Emotional abuse is confusing and complicated because it can be both verbal and actions based. It has many faces and applications. Being ignored one moment and relentlessly pursued by the same person another moment creates a form of crazy making. The victim is often driven to question their own stability.

Ultimatums are a form of emotional abuse and ought not be confused with boundaries.

Boundaries are ways to keep ourselves safe and separate from another person. We can easily envision a physical boundary. Think of a fence. What's on the inside is mine and no one is entitled to it or allowed entrance without invitation. Whatever is on the outside or other side of the fence is not mine. If someone forces themselves inside my fence or enters uninvited, I have the right to ask them to leave or have them removed. Boundaries are for us to determine and others to respect.

An ultimatum however is more of a threat. It's the "no trespassing sign under penalty of law" sign posted on the fence. It's an "or else" command. If the command is not followed, a break down in the relationship will result.

An ultimatum or emotional abuse is what preceded our family's move to Arkansas.

*Our home was stressed and filled with exhaustion. We had two young children, one dealing with a potentially chronic illness. He traveled 80-90% of the time. I was busy building a career for myself and trying to be a stay-at-home mom. Our debt was high, our patience was low. His father had just passed away. My mother was engaged to be married. Then the phone call came in.*

*A former employer wanted to re-hire my husband. They would re-instate him with full benefits, higher pay, and greater promotion potential. It was a dream come true. Yes? No. We would have to uproot our lives and move from Texas to Arkansas. To where?*

*I was a Dallas girl. I was building a business with a popular skin care company. I was glitz and glamour. We had built-in babysitters. Our church, our friends, our family. And you want me to move where?*

*I wasn't even sure our marriage would last much less survive a move to another state and away from the only support system I ever knew.*

*I asked him how bad he wanted this job. That's when he issued the ultimatum. "I want this job with or without you." Bottom line, I could move to Arkansas and stay married or I could stay in Dallas and become a single mom.*

*Did I really have a choice? The rigorously honest answer is yes, I did. It wouldn't have been easy and there is no way to predicate how our lives would have evolved. I only know when he uttered those words, I chose to go because of his threat.*

"If the wounds on her heart and the bruises on her soul were translated on her skin, you wouldn't recognize her at all." —Verona Q Maybe"

—**Barrie Davenport, Emotional Abuse Breakthrough: How to Speak Up, Set Boundaries, and Break the Cycle of Manipulation and Control with Your Abusive Partner**

## Red Rover, Red Rover

Remember the excitement and acceptance of being "the chosen one"? You were the one they believed capable to successfully steal away a member from the other team. You ran as hard and fast as you could at your assessment of their weakest link.

Then BAM! You fell backward or sometimes flew over the locked hands of those keeping you out. Not only did you let down your team, you also let yourself down. You were going to be a hero.

Yes, the games I've referenced can be simple and innocent. Unless based on other life circumstances, they simply reiterate the message we are thinking or have been told along the way. Loser. Not good enough. Weakling.

Hindsight accompanied with healthy, mature reflection can recognize that childhood games are not designed to mar our self-esteem or scar our souls. Sometimes hurt just happens.

*In my senior year of high school, I began dating a guy who was 27 years old. To be clear, I was already 18 at the time. I remember lying to my mom about his real age. My dad was a police officer and I never told him exactly how old my new boyfriend was. Since my parents were divorced, I never worried about them comparing "notes" or in this case, lies.*

*There were warning signs all along the way. If you are lying about the person you are involved with, it's a good indicator something is not right. If the age difference is unreasonable; if the other person is "separated" from a current spouse and living out of town; if they have a history of infidelity - these are indicators to RUN the other way. I was naive and thought I could get him to change his ways.*

*But "Dan" was able to take me to nice restaurants, treat me to expensive gifts, and had worldly experience that added to his charm and mystique. (In case you're wondering, no he wasn't my prom date. I lied to my friends and mom in order to skip my prom to be with him instead.)*

*We wound up dating for a total of 3 years. Not once did he ever tell one of his family members we were seeing each other. In fact, every Sunday he would call his mom from my apartment while I had to be quiet in the background so she wouldn't hear me.*

*I remember going away with him for the weekend one time. We went about four hours away to his hometown. A place out of state where he grew up and his infant daughter was being raised by his soon to be ex-wife. We ate all of our meals "to go." He wanted me to see where he was from. We drove around never stopping to visit with anyone. This was a form of emotional abuse.*

I had no idea what the signs meant.

I so desperately wanted to be loved.

I tolerated treatment I didn't deserve. I imagine you have as well.

**Here are 30 signs of emotional abuse in a relationship from Barrie Davenport:**

1. They humiliate you, put you down, or make fun of you in front of other people.

2. **They regularly demean or disregard your opinions, ideas, suggestions, or needs.**

3. They use sarcasm or "teasing" to put you down or make you feel bad about yourself.

4. **They accuse you of being "too sensitive" in order to deflect their abusive remarks.**

5. They try to control you and treat you like a child.

6. **They correct or chastise you for your behavior.**

7. You feel like you need permission to make decisions or go out somewhere.

8. **They try to control the finances and how you spend money.**

9. They belittle and trivialize you, your accomplishments, or your hopes and dreams.

10. **They try to make you feel as though they are always right, and you are wrong.**

11. They give you disapproving or contemptuous looks or body language.

12. **They regularly point out your flaws, mistakes, or shortcomings.**

13. They accuse or blame you of things you know aren't true.

14. **They have an inability to laugh at themselves and can't tolerate others laughing at them.**

15. They are intolerant of any seeming lack of respect.

16. **They make excuses for their behavior, try to blame others, and have difficulty apologizing.**

17. The repeatedly cross your boundaries and ignore your requests.

18. **They blame you for their problems, life difficulties, or unhappiness.**

19. They call you names, give you unpleasant labels, or make cutting remarks under their breath.

20. **They are emotionally distant or emotionally unavailable most of the time.**

21. They resort to pouting or withdrawal to get attention or attain what they want.

22. **They don't show you empathy or compassion.**

23. They play the victim and try to deflect blame to you rather than taking personal responsibility.

24. **They disengage or use neglect or abandonment to punish or frighten you.**

25. They don't seem to notice or care about your feelings.

26. **They view you as an extension of themselves rather than as an individual.**

27. They withhold sex as a way to manipulate and control.

28. **They share personal information about you with others.**

29. They invalidate or deny their emotionally abusive behavior when confronted.

30. **They make subtle threats or negative remarks with the intent to frighten or control you.** [*3]

The first step in recognizing emotional abuse is understanding what it is and is not. If you experience the signs of emotional abuse in your relationship, be brave and honest with yourself. Doing so, allows you to regain power over your own life.

You will be able to stop subjecting yourself to abuse and begin to heal. For those like myself who were or are minimizing, turning a blind eye, justifying, and/or covering up the abuse, this can be a painful and frightening first step.

The stress of emotional abuse will eventually catch up with your body. It takes on a variety of forms of illness. The symptoms can be easily confused or dismissed. That pain in your neck, high blood pressure, weight gain, tummy troubles, headaches. Chronic illness can be initiated from pent up feelings.

You simply can't allow it to continue, even if it means ending the relationship. A professional licensed counselor trained in abusive relationships can help you navigate the pain and fears of leaving the relationship and work with you to rebuild your self-esteem. They can provide resources for additional support as well.

I get it. As the saying goes, "Hindsight is 20/20." We can't see the forest for the trees sometimes, especially when our emotions are involved. Whether we are knowingly or naively involved in abuse, whether it is physical, verbal, or emotional, our judgment is clouded.

Do you have to have experienced a form of abuse to be hurt? I answer with a big ole' Texas-sized **NO**. Hurt producing shame and silence can take place in other forms as well.

Perhaps you may identify with one or more of the other soul scars in the next chapter. It's time to consider a broader view and range of pain and for me to introduce you to some other women and their stories.

# THE BIG "D" AND OTHER LETTERS

Up until now, I've focused on the wounds I have personally experienced. I know some of you can identify or empathize with these happenings. Others, however, may not be able to relate to forms of abuse and/or may have experienced additional hurts. By no means in order of significance, rather simply in alphabetical order, here are a few other reasons we could wear a scarlet letter or mask.

Adoption or abortion
Betrayed, body image, bullied
Contracting a sexually transmitted disease
Divorce
Exploitation
F
G

**H**
Infidelity, illness, incarcerated
**J**
**K**
Loss of a loved one through suicide
Mask of perfection
**N**
Obese
Peer abuse
**Q**
Rejection in a relationship or through loss of a job
Special needs or standing out
Terrorizing
Underweight
**V**
**W**
**X**
**Y**
**Z**

This is obviously not a complete list. You'll notice some letters have been left "blank". I invite you to connect with me to share your letter. What's **your** hurt? DaphneVSmith.com/Share

I reached out to some fellow over-comers and sisters in victory to share their stories. They've graciously and generously provided their experiences in hopes to encourage you, too, to press on.

## Adoption - Jeanna's story

Are you familiar with the musical Annie? It is the story of an orphan with plot twists, trials, and eventually triumphs. It's a happily-ever-after kind of story.

What the storyline doesn't address are the scars left on those abandoned and left for adoption, regardless of the reason or child's age.

My friend Jeanna was adopted. While going from abandoned to adopted into a new family might seem like a fairy tale come true, like the millionaire happy ending in the musical, her experience was more like a bad dream.

Yes, she was given an opportunity beyond the group home in which she been placed. However, her new family was cruel, harsh, and legalistic. She was verbally and physically abused. Punished instead of being disciplined.

Her feelings of unworthiness and being unlovable were magnified instead of soothed. Where was she to go? What was she to do? For survival, she accepted her inescapable victimhood and in time, it became comfortable and her new identity.

## Abortion - Debra's hurt

Regardless of your moral belief or opinion on abortion, it's a loss and hurt that often leads to guilt and shame. Unresolved feelings of self-condemnation can be compounded by the reason or reasons for the choice.

For Debra, those feelings included fear, abandonment, shame, condemnation, embarrassment, and being a disappointment to others. These are a few of the words she uses to describe how she felt as a result of her pregnancy termination.

Debra was (and still is) a believer with a sound network of Christian friends and a loving home. Yet, there was still a loss inside that she wanted to mask. An abortion is almost always something hidden from others. It's not something openly or casually shared.

## Being Bullied - Lisa and me

I didn't realize at the time it was happening, that I was being bullied. I was cornered in the locker room after P.E. by a group of older, taller, and intimidating girls. They were friends of someone I knew.

I was the new girl in school, easy prey, looking and longing to fit in. "Jane" tried to get me to make some wrong choices with her. I admit I made a few bad choices. But once the risk and situations started escalating beyond my comfort level, I stopped taking her calls and talking to her. As a result, she threatened to kill herself and her friends blamed me for her attempt.

I can still experience the visceral reaction I had to being surrounded. I had no idea what to do. I was scared but didn't want it to show. I took measures not be alone for the next few weeks. Thankfully, they never followed through on their threats. Yet today, more than 30 years later, I clearly see the incident if I choose to recall it.

However, my friend Lisa's bullying was internal, not external. We don't necessarily need someone else to bully us. We can literally be our own worst enemy.

With external bullies, we often have a break or relief from the attack. Once we've left their presence, while their words stay with us, at least we are out of their company.

Internal bullying, as Lisa shares, is negative self-talk and degrading. More harmful than self-deprecation, the person who bullies themselves doesn't get a break. The saying, "Wherever you go, there you are," is like shining a light on what a self-bully lives with day in and day out.

## Body Image - From the Inside Out

Too short. Too tall. Too thin. Too thick. Figure comparison is a common hurt we impose on ourselves. It's also a hurt others hurl at us through rhymes on the playground or even behind the closed doors of our homes. Sometimes they are initiated or re-enforced by our own family members.

I've always been athletically built. We just didn't call it that when I was growing up. My younger sisters were dancers; the long lean type. My maternal grandmother modeled until she was 69 years old. I can still hear her words to this day, "Daphne, you're just going to have to be on a diet every day for the rest of your life." They set the stage for decades of a self-fulling prophecy. Remember my earlier sharing about calling myself cow woman?

Her words stung and stuck. Already having developed a food addiction, it simply magnified my desire to control.

Speaking of control, Lisa assumed having a perfect body would help her be loved and accepted. Her parents' divorce is most likely where her struggle with wanting a perfect body began. She also equated love and acceptance with performance, being noticed.

When she did something fabulous such as win pageant titles, she felt like people would love her more. If she could achieve and maintain an ideal figure, surely their expression of love would be openly demonstrated or given.

## Divorce - Erica's letter

I'm talking about the big "D" and I don't mean Dallas." Yes, words to another county song. It's funny how so much of life is reflected in chart-topping lyrics. I believe it's because they're relatable. If someone else is singing about it, in some odd way it can allow us to drift away and connect to another person in the same situation. Plus, I'm originally from Texas so c'mon y'all, it's "my" music.

D-I-V-O-R-C-E. Six letters with the ability to change the lives of multiple families and generations. I've never met anyone with the intention of getting married expecting it to end in divorce. In fact, common language in a marital ceremony includes the phrase, "...until death do we part." With divorce, a death of sorts has occurred. The death of their love or unrealistic fantasy as opposed to physical parting from this world.

By no means am I judging anyone who has been divorced. Heck, each of my parents has been married three times. Because of their experiences, I know divorce can create a "scarlet letter."

I find the history of the process quite interesting though. At one point in time, women were not allowed to petition for a divorce. Once we were granted the right to petition, impotence was a legitimate just cause for the request. Before I go any farther down this slippery slope, let me get back on track.

Influenced by cultural or religious dogma, even sometimes social pressure within the couples' circle of friends, divorce can have an altering effect significantly larger than the separation of property.

Take my friend Erica for example. She was a pastor's wife. He was the one who wanted a divorce. Not only did she lose her marriage, her spiritual support changed as well. Too often clergy are considered ideal partners. Erica can attest it is far from the truth.

Being ordained is a profession not a declaration of perfection. They, too, are human and deal with everyday temptations and struggles from financial to chemical addiction, from abusive behavior to pornography.

Being a mother of five and a divorcee carried a tremendous amount of shame and guilt for Erica.

While divorce has become easier to access and facilitate over time, the pain has not lessened. Yes, there are times when a divorce is deemed appropriate or is a last hope. It could be abuse, addiction or adultery as well as the denial of or refusal to seek recovery. The damaging emotional effects are not necessarily minimized even when seemingly justified.

We are designed for relationships. When a marriage covenant is broken, the ripple effect is far reaching.

## Exploitation

Let's consider the two most popular definitions of the word exploitation:

1. the action or fact of treating someone unfairly in order to benefit from their work

2. the action of making use of and benefiting from resources

When I read those words, one name and one image comes to mind. They are Hugh Hefner and a Playboy Bunny.

I know some would argue the women who associated with and benefitted financially from their involvement did so with free will. I'm not encouraging a debate about that idea.

I am simply submitting to you for consideration - his actions were based on exploitation. I would also venture into proposing the women's families might have been hurt as well as the future relationships and job prospects for the women themselves.

I dare say the Playboy brand was the benefactor far beyond any bunny ever associated with the business.

## Mask of Perfection - Kirsten's mask

On the surface they appeared to be a "perfect" couple. A devoted wife and mother, content to serve others; a dedicated husband working with a local ministry. That's how they looked on the outside.

Everything turned inside out with the revelation of his porn addiction and her past sexual abuse. Kirsten "functioned well" for years. Dave's addiction admission blew up the walls she'd used for protection. What she didn't know at the time was the full impact her denial was taking on her physical body, mind, emotions, and spirit.

## Peer Abuse - Tiffany's hurt

Children have been playing "doctor" for decades. However, lines can get crossed during what has been labeled and accepted as normal curiosity.

Tiffany basic understanding of what was normal and safe had been skewed early on. At the early age of 5 she was sexually abused by a female peer. Tiffany felt weird and confused, and because of these feelings, she didn't know how to deal with it.

In fact, this one act of sexual abuse would set the tone for Tiffany's future relationship choices. In her words, "This one incident put me on a path of promiscuity."

As a youth, Tiffany never really understood her value or worth. Eventually, her low self-esteem and need for validation led her into a full-blown affair with a married man who was 8 years older while she was still in her late teens.

## Rejection

No one wants to be rejected, especially after having poured themselves into a job or some type of career position.

My employment history spoke for itself. I had a solid impressive track record. I would be hired to start in a certain position. I was consistently promoted within the companies I worked for without intentionally seeking a higher status.

By my late 40's I had clearly developed the entrepreneur vision. I left the standard corporate environment in lieu of creating my own brand. Admittedly I didn't have a solid vision or business plan, I simply had an idea, several certifications, and a husband who believed in me.

While I was in the development and exploration phases, we still had bills to pay. I sought a contract position with a non-profit with which I was familiar. My husband, some family members and friends had experienced a positive life change through this organization's exercises and resources.

I thought it would be both a great way to support the program and get paid in the interim. Most of the time I got to work from home with tremendous flexibility in my hours. I even got to fly out of town once a month to assist with logistics for the program.

After being in the trenches and having a behind-scenes understanding of the day-to-day operations, I realized there were some ways to address inefficiencies; eventually resulting in decreased expenses and a more streamlined customer experience.

I pitched my ideas to a co-worker and got genuine support and encouragement to present the concepts to the owners. My initial presentation was apparently appreciated and well-received. I was excited about the possibility of making a real impact for the organization.

A few days passed. While my co-worker and I awaited the green light, I noticed I began having computer issues. Certain records were no longer available to me. We had a history of challenges with various platforms so it was more frustrating than concerning.

One day out of the blue, I received a call. Both owners wanted to talk to me. They said since I wasn't happy with the way things were structured and clearly not interested in the status quo, I was being let go immediately. "Pack up your computer and send it back today."

I had given my heart and soul to that group. I went as far as taking only one day off during the weekend of my grandfather's funeral in order to be available to support the program. Once the initial shock wore off, I was devastated. I had never been "let go" before. It was simply unbelievable to me.

I was bombarded by questions and inquiries for months after my dismissal by volunteers still serving the organization. Apparently, no explanation was given as to my exit. I didn't want to get into mud-slinging or slander. I simply redirected people with needs to the appropriate parties and tried to maintain my dignity.

I had never experienced a rejection or termination in employment. I was left hurt, devastated, and grieving.

## Singleness AND Rejection - Dalia's pain

Coupled, paired, two by two; it dates farther back than Noah and the ark. We are "supposed" to be partnered. In certain cultures and based on archaic customs and assumptions, being a single woman in your 30s can be a stigma.

This is part of Dalia's pain.

She craved to be coupled so much so her focus was on being pursued. Her end goal, her only goal, was to be married.

Never feeling wanted by her parents, being desired by a man who would love and cherish her as his wife was something she longed for. Being married would signify a man's approval of her, right? At least at the time and in her mind it did. Being single for decades starting messing with her emotions and she began to base her value on someone else's acceptance or lack thereof.

What was "wrong" with her that no prince had proposed? Why was she still alone?

These stories are real.

These are women I know, care for and admire.

Their hurts have been worn as both scarlet letters and or masks in order to hide the pain. Sometimes visible, like Hester's; other times, hidden.

As our journey continues, you'll hear more from these women.

My hope at this juncture is for you to have recognized your hurts and possibly connected with someone in this book who has encountered the same type of pain or shared circumstances.

I want you to know you're not alone. There is hope.

The first step to healing is admitting our pain. It's not a sign of weakness. It's a sign of strength.

Strong women admit they've been hurt. They're willing to say, "STOP! I'll not hide or take it any longer."

Join me as we get real with ourselves and begin the transformation to freedom from our scarlet letters and masks to claiming and owning our value and victory.

What are the scarlet letters you've been wearing?

# HEALING YOUR HURT

Before we can release, we must first recognize.

We never know what might be going on behind the scenes with colleagues, friends, or sadly within our own family. Most often, people put on their happy face and plunge into the day simply trying to not draw suspicion and avoid further hurt. I did.

For decades I lived numb. I didn't want to feel or realize the full implication or impact of what I had experienced. I reasoned, as long as I kept everything in the dark, didn't acknowledge I had been hurt or made poor choices, then maybe, it didn't really happen.

Through recovery resources, therapy, and experiential programs, I've come to realize I was also living in denial. I also realized I didn't want to live that way any longer.

So far, we've recognized external scars are not a prerequisite to trauma. Internal scars can bare even greater pain. That's a lot to process and consider. As you've picked up, this is not a "light read." Neither is what you have gone through or may still be going through. My goal for this book and process are to shed light into the lies of the dark and to lighten your burdens.

If you're ready, it's time recognize your hurts. It's time to admit your pain.

But before we move on, let's put all of the cards are on the table.

Some guidelines I recommend include:

- Be gentle with yourself
- Try not to judge yourself
- Allow your thoughts and feelings to arise organically. No need to create an accurate timeline.
- Trust, there is light on the other side of the dark.

This first exercise is designed to be completed in a safe secure place, during a period without a tight time constraint. In other words, sitting in the carpool line, at a doctor's appointment or during a "quick" break from work are not ideal scenarios.

In addition to time, you need a couple of old school tools - something to write on and something to write with. I suggest using paper, be it loose leaf, a journal, or notebook of some type. I do encourage you to select something you are willing to dispose of later. Let's just say, there may or may not be some fire involved.

Once we let them go, we want them fully released, not hanging around collecting dust or perhaps discovered by someone at a later date. Unless of course you choose to write an entire book about your experiences, you know like some people. Come on, if we don't start to lighten up, we're going to continue to stay down.

If you choose to use a computer device of some kind, keep in mind that more than once in history information has been discovered and leaked through this medium. In my opinion, good old paper and pen allow for the most flexibility, adaptability and security.

You may choose to process one hurt at a time and that's okay. There is no "right" way to experience your feelings. You are neither good nor bad for having these feelings and no feeling is either good or bad. They simply are.

Take a big deep breath. Now exhale and let's get started.

You've carried these hurts for too long. It's time to begin your transformation to freedom.

1.  What is the first memory of being hurt that pops into your mind? Be as detailed as possible. (Include who, where, what, and when.)

2.  What were the physical or visceral reactions you experienced or may still have upon recall?

3.  What were the emotions or feelings you felt as the hurt was taking place?

4.  What was your part in the hurt? (Note: If you were abused, especially as a child, you have no part. It happened to you not because of you.)

5. How did what happened affect you today?

6. What lies do you believe about yourself because of the hurt?

Well done!

You have taken a HUGE step toward releasing the burdens you've carried. Be proud of yourself. It takes tremendous strength and courage to admit our hurts. By hanging in there up to now, you've already broken a link, or maybe many more, in the chain that has been keeping you bound.

This might be a new place for you, even new feelings.

For some, you may still feel a bit numb. Others might experience more intense feelings of hurt and shame by reliving the trauma.

Or perhaps your head and heart feel clearer. More energy is flowing through you and there's a glow behind your eyes. It's because you are seeing things in a new way. You feel released from hiding the secrets.

Healing is a process and it takes time.

While the hurt may have been a one-time event, you've probably carried it for an extended period of time. If the violation was carried on for days, weeks, or years, we can't expect to wave a magic wand and make it disappear.

Trust me, you're already on your way. Press on and press through. There is joy awaiting you on the other side of your past.

To encourage and support you to press on, I've included some of my favorite references for strength and release. I'm excited to continue this journey with you.

## References for Strength and Release

Then Jesus said, "Come to me, all of you who are weary and carry heavy burdens, and I will give you rest." – Matthew 11:28 (NLT)

"Then you will know the truth, and the truth will set you free." – John 8:32 (NIV)

We all face difficult times and trials. We must never lose hope.

"It is our wounds that create in us a desire to reach for miracles." – Jocelyn Soriano

Pain is inevitable. Misery is optional.

"When someone stabs you it's not your fault that you feel pain." – Louise Penny

"It's a lot easier to be angry at someone than it is to tell them you're hurt." – Zakiya Caswell

"Being hurt by someone you truly care about leaves a hole in your heart that only love can fill." – George Bernard Shaw

"Some people use their own hurt as an excuse for hurting others." – Roland Merullo

"Being brokenhearted is like having broken ribs. On the outside it looks like nothing's wrong, but every breath hurts." – Greg Behrendt

"Pain can be endured and defeated only if it is embraced. Denied or feared, it grows." – Dean Koontz

When Jesus saw him and knew he had been ill for a long time, He asked him, "Would you like to get well?" – John 5:6 (NLT)

"The most terrifying thing is to accept oneself completely." —Carl Jung

"The weak can never forgive. Forgiveness is the attribute of the strong." —Mahatma Gandhi

"You can't heal a wound by saying it's not there!" – Jeremiah 6:14 (TLB)

When the pain of holding on is greater than the fear of letting go, you're ready to start healing.

"He will not break the bruised reed, nor quench the dimly burning flame. He will encourage the fainthearted, those tempted to despair. He will see full justice given to all who have been wronged." – Isaiah 42:3 (TLB)

# RELEASE YOUR SHAME

*Guilt is thinking and feeling I did wrong.*
*Shame is thinking and feeling I am wrong.*

# SHAME SHAME GO AWAY

Shame. It ought to be a four letter word. It adds insult to injury.

There are two types of shame - healthy and unhealthy.

Healthy shame is when we feel guilt for an act in which we caused another person harm. It's an internal alarm, if you will. It's a gut check to help us comprehend the difference between right and appropriate or harmful and inappropriate choices. When we break an agreement with someone, hurt someone's feelings, or feel embarrassed, these are examples of healthy shame. A moral violation is another example of healthy shame.

Healthy shame is good. It allows us to grow from our experiences, learn, make amends, and live together with care and compassion. It's a distinguishing characteristic amongst healthy normal human beings.

Unhealthy shame, on the other hand, is when we allow an act to make us feel condemned or to define us. Condemnation is different than conviction. Conviction allows us to be aware of a mistake or error, driving us to change our behavior and choices in the future. It's our inner program, our moral compass, encouraging correction or re-enforcing character.

Condemnation on the other hand attacks our personal character, our inner most being, our confidence and self-esteem. It chips away at our value and worth, sometimes silently and slowly causing a fade in what was once a bright light. It's an indicator of the power of unhealthy shame.

Unhealthy shame causes us to create further injury and prolong the pain. It drives us to either replay or repress memories. It's the kind of shame that forces us to keep our mouth shut, go numb, and take false ownership of something someone else did to us.

Physical symptoms of unhealthy shame manifest themselves in a variety of ways:

- nausea
- addiction
- self-attack or injury (including cutting, bulimia and other harmful actions)
- heaviness in the chest
- poor eye contact and slow speech patterns
- body minimizing (like slumped shoulders and a hanging the head)
- even low energy.

Emotional symptoms include sadness, depression, lone-liness, and self-loathing. Those harboring unhealthy shame can also become angry and project their shame onto others through attack.

I am not a medical doctor and these symptoms are not meant to diagnose. My intention is to shed light and expand awareness. I encourage you to seek professional qualified medical treatment if needed.

Once we identify and let go of unhealthy shame, our hurts can be more easily healed. While perhaps they are never forgotten, they can at least be forgiven. Forgiveness is for the forgiver. It brings relief to us and lightens our burden.

Forgiveness is like a bath; without it life stinks AND most likely, once is not enough. We can begin to hold our head a little higher, rest a little easier, and venture into the process of loving ourselves with grace when we begin to forgive.

There is hope for gaining peace with our past, no lon-ger allowing it to define our present or determine our potential.

Here's an interesting fact - babies don't blush.

They have no natural sense of embarrassment. They don't feel self-conscious or shame. Let's consider a baby's first few years of life. They poop and pee on themselves without care or concern. They fall down when they first learn to walk. They have no sense of right or wrong until they learn it.

Our experiences and those who care for us teach us the differences between healthy and unhealthy shame. When our wires get crossed, it's an opportunity for conviction to gain a toehold and begin spreading like an infectious disease or plague.

Let's consider the source or sources of our shame before we "should" on ourselves any longer. Did we have healthy moral models in the beginning? Have our views been infiltrated by others? What and where do our heart and gut guide us?

# IT WASN'T YOUR FAULT

One of the challenges with hurt and shame can come from an unexpected event in and of itself. Sometimes it's a subtle assault. Other times, it happens shockingly and out of the blue.

Let's talk about subtle assaults first. They can be hard to determine and that is one of their more prevalent characteristics. This is one of the crazy-making aspects of the assault. Movies and media lead us to believe graphic, heinous offenses define abuse. While yes, this is often the case, it's not always the case.

I have never personally been threatened at gunpoint, had acid thrown on me, been part of a sex-trafficking ring. I've not experienced what could be described as a "major" change incident. Most of my hurt and shame were slow fades, subtle assaults that chipped away at my soul and sanity. These attacks can also be known as grooming.

When we are born, we are innately scared of two things: falling and loud noises. All of the other fears we have in life are learned. Are you familiar with the term "childlike innocence?" It's this innocence or lack of fear that predators and perpetrators prey on when they are grooming someone to be a victim.

*Every eight minutes, a child is sexually assaulted in the U.S.[1], and 93 percent know the perpetrator[2]. Many perpetrators of sexual abuse are in a position of trust or responsible for the child's care, such as a family member, teacher, clergy member, or coach. (RAINN.org)*

*In its most simple definition, sexual assault or abuse is any type of sexual activity that a person does not agree to. (Women's health.gov) The term molestation refers to a young child being perpetrated.*

With grooming, an adult caregiver, mentor, coach, teacher and the list can go on, earns the trust of their victim. Often it is automatically through a common interest or position of leadership and authority. They provide extra encouragement and attention to the child in order to make them feel special. A secret bond is often formed.

Because the child has been singled out in a positive way, the offender now has some leverage. A desensitizing begins. It can start with secret communication through texts and other sources of messaging. **PARENTS - this is why we need password access to our children's accounts.**

Then they slowly begin to push the boundaries from a parting hug or thank you pat on the back, arm, etc to a more surprising and advanced interaction as time goes on.

What is a child to do? If threats are part of the equation, the victim is caught between a rock and a hard place. Do they dare tell and risk whatever harm has been promised if they do so? Do they continue to endure, hoping it will stop or be found out? Can they trust they will be listened to?

What happens when someone is violated at such a young age that their voice or sense of right and wrong hasn't been fully developed? Tiffany and I both encountered this interruption in our development. Tiffany by a peer, mine by an adult.

Let's pause for a moment and think about a young child. Often, they have difficulty communicating their needs and desires for simple things such as food, naps, toys, and so on. Verbal skills and accurate usage of vocabulary takes time, often years. Five years of age is on the early side of becoming proficient in self-expression.

Our inner voice begins developing at the onset of birth. When that voice is interrupted during development it causes a "kink" in our mind and development. Until a child reaches a certain age, they are not yet capable of identifying whether a person is good, bad, or both.

Self-doubt is internal crazy-making. When we can't trust ourselves, how can we trust others?

Grooming often leads to decades of doubt in a person's own value. It can set someone up to question their identity and most certainly leads to the questioning of one's own judgment when it comes to trusting others.

As we mature and if we've become attuned to self-awareness instead of having it interrupted, our intuition can guide us through career choices, dating opportunities, financial planning, and other life decisions.

Our self-awareness can include what is commonly known as "gut instinct." How about taking that last bite of dessert? It's a literal gut check. "I knew I should have skipped that last spoonful." Our inner voice deserves to be heeded.

Our guts are designed for more than processing food. They help us process our feelings as well. Several years ago an acronym came to me. In my mind, gut stands for God's Urging To. It's an internal prompting designed to guide us.

If our instincts can help us avoid a traffic jam because we had a "gut feeling" to take a different route, they can also serve as a red flag, warning flare, firework or whatever other image gets your attention. How about the expression, "I knew in my gut something was wrong." Or "Something just didn't feel right. It didn't sit well in my gut."

However, when that intuition has not been allowed to develop in a healthy, safe, natural process, the results can be long-lasting, creating a veiled self-doubt about the validity or actuality of perpetration.

After the Harvey Weinstein case made international news, actress Alyssa Milano started a movement that went viral. She encouraged everyone who had been assaulted to simply post #metoo in their social media status. Thousands of men, yes men, and women from around the world came forward. Personal friends and family of mine stepped out of the dark and into the healing and empowerment of light.

I clearly remember one friend posting, "Does age 8 count?" I simply replied to her post, "Any age counts."

Our best defense is to teach our children and listen to their gut, to trust themselves. If something doesn't seem or "feel" right, most likely it isn't! If you are a parent reading this, listen to YOUR gut. If something doesn't seem right with your child, if they have slowly or suddenly changed, check it out. You're not being nosey.

Ask questions.

Trust your child.

As long as a secret remains in the dark, it has power over us.

**Anyone who has been groomed needs to realize it was not their fault.** They do not have to own any blame or shame. I'm not saying it will be easy to release the unhealthy shame. Heck, I know from personal experience it won't be.

We also need to know grooming can take place at any age. "Adult grooming is correspondent to child grooming and applies to any situation where an adult is primed to allow him or herself to be exploited or abused." [*4]

Who are the victims of grooming? Men. Women. Children. Young adults. The middle-aged. The elderly. The lonely and the emotionally compromised. Those whose defenses are down. Anyone with soft boundaries. In short: There is no prototypical victim. Almost anyone can be vulnerable to grooming. Predators are practiced and extremely good at what they do. Those who are not, tend to get caught. Those who get caught, tend to learn from their mistakes and refine their techniques. You don't have to be especially gullible to fall victim to grooming, but if you learn the signs, you can successfully identify a potential abuser, and avoid exploitation.

Predators work in the shadows and have something to hide.

Predators claim to feel a "special connection" with their targets, even if they've only just met.

Predators recruit co-conspirators (forced teaming) to fight their battles and do their bidding.

Predators draw their victims in by sharing private information then swearing them to secrecy.

Predators practice divide-and-conquer techniques in order to manipulate others.[*5]

Education, communication, and interaction can minimize the effects of grooming. Sadly, I'm not sure it will ever be eliminated. We live in a society where we must have a certain level of trust with others. Background checks can help minimize exposure and provide a barrier of protection. However, as long as humans have a sin nature, it's going to happen somewhere, sometime to someone. We must live alert.

I am encouraging a healing process beginning with giving ourselves grace and compassion. What choice did you truly have? I dare advocate, you didn't "allow" it. It happened to you not because of you.

From a slow fade to a shocking assault, either way it can be hard to believe.

In hind sight, I too often tried to rationalize what happened to me. "What did I do to provoke it?" "That was so out of his character. Maybe it was my fault." "Surely I misunderstood."

Does any of that sound familiar?

For some of us, after decades of seeking permission or trying to please others, we really don't know how to listen to ourselves or distinguish the difference between what we want and what others want for us or from us. One of my favorite tools learned on my journey of recovery is an expression, "Don't should on yourself." This is especially empowering for recovering people pleasers and victims of grooming.

How do we help minimize future or end current perpetrations? It starts with talking about it. It comes from trusting your gut, your inner voice.

"Did that really just happen?" "Am I being too sensitive?" Whether it was isolated or repeated, subtle or not. If your gut felt it, then take heed.

Hurt ranging from assault to abuse, proposition to rape, can be physical or emotional. Grooming permeates both boundaries. Once unhealthy shame has crept in, it takes extraordinary strength to replace it with truth and the realization of our truly value and worth.

Unhealthy shame in and of itself is a predator. It grooms it's victims to doubt themselves, to discount their rights and discourage their boundaries. It's a parasite that fills and fuels itself on lies. Once exposed, however, the lies begin to lose their power.

# EXPOSING THE LIES

From **Tiffany** - While not all of her relationships were sexual, she began to believe a lie of the enemy which shouted, "You can't keep a boyfriend unless you have sex with him…"

This and many other lies from the enemy began to birth stress and anxiety within Tiffany's heart, ultimately resulting in insecurity.

Tiffany was emotionally broken, and as a result, she took these beliefs into her marriage. Because of the insecurity, hurt, pain, rejection, and the lies of the enemy Tiffany put a lot of unnecessary pressure on her husband to be perfect. This was unfair both to him and their marriage, and it ultimately caused major marital problems.

**Kirsten** lived in a prison of lies. As the warden and lead architect of this prison, she- carefully constructed it over many years. Regularly reinforcing, patching up and reinforcing it again to protect herself from further hurt. She thought the lies were for her protection and the protection of others. She believed the lies would maintain her self-image and bolster her self-esteem. Eventually, however, she lost track of all the distortions and became weary from the weight of carrying them.

The lies she believed were like tapes stored in her mind and set on auto-replay. Regularly, they reminded her of all she needed to protect in order to maintain her image and to give herself value. Some of the messages were clever, being only one degree off of the truth. But, they were still lies. White lies- lies meant to soften the blow and save face.

The messages she replayed in her head included:

> Don't think. Don't feel. Don't remember.
> Stay in the shadows.
> Forget and keep moving on.
> Hide.
> Be a tough girl.

"In many ways, I felt like everyone knew the lie we'd been living. I felt like a pariah, an outcast. I was so afraid that if anyone took the time to really look in my eyes, they would see the guilt, the shame I was trying to hide. While I didn't have a scarlet -"A"'- embroidered on my shirt, it felt like a neon sign that flashed -"'imposter'"- incessantly above both of us. And once the story came out, I was certain we would be destroyed. Therefore, I carefully reinforced my protective walls. I couldn't be discovered. I had to protect myself at all costs." - excerpted from *Choosing a Way Out*

**Dalia** never felt wanted by anyone. When we seek other people's approval the common lie is we're not good enough, especially for a committed long term relationship. We're disposable and only good for right now.

**Lisa** would perform well or did something fabulous, then she felt like people would love her. She thought she had to earn love. From achievement to physical appearance, she pursued perfection more for acceptance and approval of others than for her own personal satisfaction. She believed the lie, performance = love.

**Debra** believed the lie she would forever be under the guilt of the abortion. Later in life, she gave birth to two other children. One was stillborn and her second passed away an hour after birth. The guilt from her abortion intensified as she experienced the additional loss of these two sons. She wondered…was this a consequence for her abortion years earlier? The biggest lie of all was she could never be completely forgiven by God. She knew in her head He still loved her but in heart she felt that sin would always be a dividing line. She tried to hide from the lies behind a mask.

**Erica** believed others were judging and looking down on her. She believed she wore a scarlet D on her chest and that label defined her. She could actually feel pity. Being now a former pastor's wife, she felt ashamed and hopeless in the presence of her church "family." In her pain she cried out, "God, please help me see myself the way You see me and help me to forgive myself and to receive Your unmerited grace. I desperately need You to teach me how to love myself as a divorced person. I need to embrace Your love for me. Help me to see that

Your love will cast out all my fear and anger and any title that I am now given."

"Over the years I heard people say, 'God is my husband,' but after reading and rereading that Scripture, it finally became a revelation and a reality in my life. God really was my husband. We really were a whole family. My kids did have a Father, a perfect Father who would never leave them nor forsake them. God promised me that I did not have to be ashamed about my situation anymore. Nor was I an outcast to society. Being divorced did not define who I really was. You do not have to live with the label D on your chest. Divorce does not define you. Once I finally grasped and really understood that God is my husband and that He unconditionally loved me…faults and all…that was when I started forgetting the shame of my singleness and abandonment. I started embracing myself in a healthier way. Slowly, I began to accept my singleness instead of hiding from it."

**Jeanna** believed that she was no good, unlovable, and had no value. Perhaps the most extraordinary lie of all - she was full of the devil. She believed she didn't deserve happiness, security, or acceptance.

I remember the first time I heard Elsa sing these words in the movie Frozen, "Don't let them in.

Don't let them see. Be the good girl you always have to be. Conceal, don't feel. Don't let them know." Something resonated deep within my soul.

Then the crescendo, "Let it go. Let it go…I don't care what they're going to say."

It only takes a hairline fracture in the mask or letter we bear to allow the lies to be dispelled. Sometimes it requires someone else coming forward to share their pain, their experience with the lies, in order for us to gain awareness.

When Harvey Weinstein, Larry Nasser, and Jerry Sandusky were at the height of their reigns of terror, their victims concealed, they hid. They kept quiet out of fear. Each of these men abused their power through threats of damaging the future career and goal accomplishments of the women and children they abused.

Consider Olympic gold medalist Aly Raisman as well as the hundreds of young women who trusted Dr. Larry Nasser. The families of his patients made sacrifices in order to support their daughter's dreams, hopes, and talents. Not only were the athletes violated, I believe their families were assaulted as well.

These predators and perpetrators sicken me. They abused their position to provide care and opportunity for those who trusted and, at least at first most likely, admired these men. They lied and manipulated people and situations in order to feed their own sick needs.

Once these men began their abuse, I have no doubt those they preyed on felt trapped. We're talking "captains" in their industries. Experts who were highly revered for their accomplishments and connections. They held the keys to unlock doors and opportunities for those who had put their trust in them.

What is a person to do, regardless if they are a legal adult or still a child? Who do they turn to? Who do they confide in? Who will believe them? Why must it take decades and legions of casualties for there to be an investigation?

In part, it's because of the fear created by the lies and threats imposed. "Oh, I was only kidding." "What!? I would never do or say such a thing." "Do you know who I am and what I can do to your future?"

The person who risks exposing their offender has courage and strength paralleled to a super power. They have hope beyond themselves; breaking their silence by sharing, not only will their terror end but perhaps they can spare another from the same fate.

All those who sent out #metoo through social media channels considered others as or even more valuable than themselves. They refused to allow another innocent person to be violated. They stood up and spoke out refusing to be a silent, suffering slave to the lies.

They were sick and tired of being sick and tired. Whether it was continual abuse or a single isolated incident, shining the light into the darkness was the beginning of the end of the power of the lies.

# WHAT IF IT ONLY HAPPENED ONCE?

I remember my days of ignorance and judgement.

"How could she subject herself to that repeated abuse?"

"Once is all it would take for me to leave."

"Why does she put up with that? I would never let anyone talk to me that way."

I shudder when I consider that I ever criticized someone, even in thought alone.

How does anyone really know if once would be enough? Yet, what if it was only once? Is that reason enough to leave the relationship, report the incident, risk an investigation? The possible upset of families, careers, entire lifestyles including a potential change in homes, schools, even jobs are at stake.

These are serious considerations each woman needs to assess and decide on her own. The urging of a well-intended friend or family member who may or may not have an agenda or is able to relate based on their own experiences can be one type of resource. Seeking a trained professional's expert and non-biased guidance is another variable in the equation to consider when making a possible life-altering decision. The ultimate decision to stop, to break away, almost always comes down to an individual's choice. When is enough, enough?

As I shared in my introduction, I remember the exact day my switch flipped. Try as I might prior to that day, my head and heart had not yet been in alignment. When I made the decision to bring an end to our accustomed pattern, I had the resolve, regardless of the outcome, that things were no longer going to be accepted as status quo.

But let me back up. Once is one time too many. The veil of innocence is torn with the very first offense. And once it has been torn, it does not justify a bigger deeper tear. We need to eliminate the word "just" from these scenarios. It "just happened once". He "just over-reacted." I "just pushed him too far." The word "just" minimizes reality.

*It was a Friday evening and we just arrived home from a family night at a local pizza and game place. Yes, we were both stressed and tired. Two demanding careers, two kids-one with a chronic health issue. Well past bedtime, we had all hit the wall with patience.*

*The tension rose over something as silly and insignificant as water on the kitchen countertop.*

*When our daughter started whining about wanting to go see her grandmother, it was the straw that broke the camel's back. In frustration and exhaustion, my husband scooped her up in his arms and headed to the top of the stairs.*

*I panicked. Maybe I'd seen one too many soap operas. Maybe it was my fight or flight instinct. Whatever it was, I was driven to pursue him. I was about two steps behind him when I lunched to grab his shirt and stop him.*

*He set our daughter down. He turned toward me. There was a look in his eye I'd never seen before. It felt like he'd grown a foot taller and I had shrunk both in years and inches.*

*I walked backward down the stairs and into the foyer. My back was literally against the wall; that's when it happened.*

*He hit me, in the face. Was it a fist or a slap? Does it truly matter? My world has just been blown open. I had never even been so much as spanked when I was a child much less struck.*

*I was shaking. I was scared. I had no idea what would, could or should happen next.*

*I grabbed my cell phone, ran to the bathroom, and called the police.*

*"911, what's your emergency?" "My husband just hit me." (At that very moment I realized, we had just become a statistic.)*

*It was truly incredulous and surreal.*

*I knew when he got angry, he had a temper.*

*Up until now, I had never experienced it at this level. In the past he'd yell or totally shut down. This was a new side of him I'd never seen before.*

*By the time the officers arrived, he had cooled down. So much so, he didn't understand why I called them. He'd gone back to cleaning the kitchen.*

*Was it black out anger? Was it denial? Whatever it was, there was no excuse- only evidence and damage.*

*I chose to take the children and leave our home that night. We stayed gone for a couple of days. I was scared and shell shocked. I tried to carry on as "normal" as possible. We made it an adventure to stay at grandma's.*

*One Monday morning, our son, still in diapers, had gone through what I had taken with us the night we left. Cloth diapers weren't easy to come by so I went back to the house for a fresh supply. I waited until I thought he would be at work.*

*I remember walking through the front door to a dark, curtain-drawn living room. He sat there, quiet, still. A depression had come over him. He realized he may have lost everyone and everything because he had lost control.*

*I pushed for counseling, again, and he obliged. But, we never dealt with his root issues. It would take another 15 years of marriage and a different family crisis to start the healing process for his anger and for me to feel truly safe enough to be fully vulnerable again.*

A one-time incident, however, creates an opening to allow a second time. Like weeds growing in the cracks of a sidewalk, the occurrences spread until our entire path is now stained with blemishes caused by assault, abuse, and/or attack.

For those like myself who were assaulted and betrayed at a young age, it can be hard to imagine a life where it has never happened. A life free of berating comments, forced actions, physical lines crossed. At times realizing there are people in the world who have never been violated can be unfathomable. Sadly, I cannot begin to relate or understand that type of insulation. Most likely, neither can you and that's why you're still reading this book and are willing to consider a change.

I wrote this book, in part, for those who need to be set free from their hurts and shame as well as a possible warning to those who have not been assaulted. It may serve as a tool to learn what to be aware of in future relationships and situations. It might also serve as a resource or conversation starter with someone you know.

Whether you're reading this book because you have personally been attacked or because someone you know and love is experiencing assault, any single act of abuse is excessive. When I looked up abuse in the dictionary, an initial definition was physical maltreatment. I dug deeper and came across words and phrases like misuse, cruel or violent treatment, to use for a bad purpose. To me, those are more relatable. I can identify more with those concepts.

Even if I had never been violated as a child, each isolated incident during my teen and early adulthood were enough to qualify as either abuse, assault or attack. Too often, with subtle assault or random, one-time incidents and the absence of excessive external bruising or broken bones, the offense is discounted or diminished. It was a "misunderstanding." It was blown "out of proportion." These are classic phrases either thought or at times spoken out loud by a victim, especially when questioned by someone.

Does any of this sound sickeningly familiar?

There's also the instance and confusion of blackout anger. Once a blow up has occurred the one who blew up can't seem to remember what even happened, leaving us to wonder if we made it up or misunderstood. Did what just happen, *really* happen?

Rarely are there witnesses and in possibly the worst case, children observed the incident. How do we always know if it was real or if our minds are playing tricks on us or we're over-exaggerating?

*Yes, I stood up for myself during a heated argument. No, shoving me in response was not an appropriate reaction.*

*I was tempted to justify it. "If only I hadn't talked back. If only I had tried harder to keep the peace." At that point, the damage was done. My daughter fled from the room. I went after her. There was no denying her upset state. There was no explaining it away. All I could do was apologize to her for allowing her to be in the crossfire. No. That's not all I could do. I could also begin the journey out of denial and allow healing and truth to replace decades of verbal bullying.*

*I recall an incident that took place about 20 years earlier involving that same daughter.*

*I was laying down on the couch with our infant baby girl sleeping on my chest. Earlier that day my husband and I had attended a therapy session. He came home upset from work that evening. I was told if I didn't like the way things were going, I could leave. "Pack up your stuff and get out. Leave the credit cards and take the baby." I was stunned. I had never been given an ultimatum like that before. I couldn't fully process what was being said. Or should I say how I was being threatened?*

*Even with a local support system of family and friends, I had no idea what to do. I had no job. I loved this man who just blew up at me. We had a baby. I had little girl princess dreams. My prince had turned on me and my fairy godmother was nowhere in sight. I emotionally withdrew and did what I thought I needed to do to keep the peace and not cause any more upset. This was actually a skill I had begun developing growing up in an alcoholic environment. If I was a good enough girl, maybe I wouldn't cause anyone to be mad or yell.*

*A sincere apology from him and my desire to keep our marriage together resulted in unresolved hurt feelings and resentment that I carried for years. Until that day when my flip switched.*

*I now understand. The bullying had been going on for decades. It was a subtle assault.*

My inability to not stand up for myself, my desire to keep the peace at all costs, to go along with things I didn't agree with were all signs of codependency. In addition I had been harmed or damaged from the sexual encounters that had taken place for decades, dating back to the first perpetration at the hands of my caregiver.

In my story, each assault or abuse happened just once. No two were ever the same. They wove together forming a strand of lies and misconceptions about what was appropriate, what was acceptable and normal, and what crossed the line. That's why it was so easy to dismiss or justify.

To answer my own question posed at the beginning of this chapter, yes, once is enough. And, one time is too many.

What if I drank poison only one time? Would that count? Would it hurt me in some way?

Believing we deserve the abuse or the offender is justified is sipping slowly on the poison of shame.

# NO EXCUSE FOR ABUSE

If what happened to you never resulted in a call to the police or a trip to the emergency room, was it *REALLY* that big of a deal?

Simply answered - YES.

Are the possible consequences of breaking the silence worth the possible ramifications?

That's another resounding - YES.

Assault is assault whether the result is internal or external bruising, charges filed or closed confession, industry "leader" or "boy" next door. Whether it was a one-time isolated incident or insidiously repeated. Regardless of witnesses or not, if it was traumatic to you, it's a big deal.

Merriam-Webster defines a big deal as something of special importance. My view is this - if I would be appalled or enraged at the very thought of the offense in question happening to my daughter, sister, niece, or friend, then it's a big deal.

Regardless of how we grew up, how our mothers were spoken to, what happened to our friend at their house, certain things are just wrong. Your wellness, safety, and value deserve to be honored. If they are not, it's a big deal.

Herein lies a challenge with certain assaults - they are often overlooked because they were "only" one time occurrences or because they didn't leave any visible scaring. Another possible reason to dismiss an incident is the continual slow fade I've mentioned. Maybe it was a case of grooming as shared earlier.

**Just because something is familiar, doesn't make it okay.**

Just because something is familiar, doesn't make it okay. A certain amount of resolution must take place in order to survive in an environment where there is no apparent way of escape. It doesn't mean the victim actually accepts or agrees with the treatment. It means they are fighting for survival to the best of their current ability. Denial or diminishing becomes a coping mechanism. Making excuses and accepting blame are definite signs of abuse.

If you are in an actively abusive relationship, your immediate safety is the number one priority. If you choose to leave that situation, please do so with the assistance of a professional or organization that will guide you through the process.

We each have our own individual pain tolerance, be it physical or emotional. What would cause one person to put an immediate end to a certain treatment or behavior is not the same for someone else. It took me decades to draw a line. In the end, hurt may need to boil down to an individual assessment.

### WARNING: Soapbox Moment!

*I believe our society has become somewhat immune or desensitized to what is appropriate, safe, and healthy.*

*We began as a puritan society; covering our bodies from head to toe and not speaking of "such things" even like menopause with other women. While that may not have been ideal, we've gone to the total extreme of baring it all in public and advertising sexual performance and pleasure enhancements on television! And I'm not talking about only on cable.*

*Don't get me started about what's available on and through the internet.*

*Could it be that all of access contributes to the confusion about what is appropriate and what is not? Have we grown numb from repeated exposure and shock?*

*I could also launch into a diatribe about "no" meaning no. The first time it is spoken, it needs to shut-down any further actions. "No" is not to be challenged or questioned.*

*Okay, stepping down from the box. End of rant. I share my opinions and beliefs in order to convey my concern about how easy it is to get confused about blurred boundaries.*

Bottom line - regardless of the number of incidents or the perpetrator, was a visceral reaction experienced either during or after the assault?

I also want to be very clear here, I'm not talking about regret. We need to recognize there are times we've all thought back and wished we'd made a different choice. Maybe I went "too far" or farther than I intended because I got caught up in the moment. Perhaps alcohol was involved and if we could rewind the clock and have a different outcome that left our dignity in-tact, we would.

There are a few guys and times in my past where I've wondered, 'Were they abusers or simply jerks?'

*I remember this guy who knew I was head over heels for him. Instead of admitting he was no longer interested in seeing me, he lied about his family moving out of the area. I was devastated. My mom still remembers hearing me crying out loud all the way across the house when he gave me the news. And yes, you guessed it. They never moved and I'm pretty convinced there was never a plan to do so. I would call that being a weak jerk, not emotional abuse.*

*Then there was the guy who acted like a friend. He showed compassion and interest in me that was strictly platonic. I felt comfortable around him and enjoyed talking with him. My boyfriend at the time swore this guy had ulterior motives. The minute my boyfriend and I broke up, this "friend" swooped in to make his move. Again, by in my judgement this "friend" was being a jerk not an abuser.*

Please keep in mind, not every upsetting or unexpected interaction falls under the category of assault or abuse.

We also need to be aware there are those who manipulate and lie. They have remorse after an event and try to blame or accuse the other party. This is a feeling of guilt or embarrassment for having participated in something they wish they could erase.

Synonyms for the word *perpetrate* include effect, inflict, wreak, commit. If they describe the act that took place, to me it's a big deal. Regret is a different situation all together.

Right here, right now, before we go any farther, let me make something very clear. There is a difference between assault and manipulation. While some might think it obvious, I've learned to never assume. This book has been inspired by, written for, and dedicated to those who have innocently been assaulted, abused, and taken advantage of.

Sometimes an incident, or series of incidents, produces an initial shock or a shut-down out of self-protection. The gut-wrenching, heat-inducing, crawly-skin feeling may only happen upon recalling the hurt, maybe hours, days, months, or years later. If those types of feelings occur, then yes, it was a big deal.

Prison cells are filled with countless innocent people who have been wrongly accused out of vengeance, jealousy, and other heinous motives by conniving individuals. I am deeply saddened when the systems established to protect are used for fraud.

Seducing and lying are an abomination. We all must, and at some point will, experience the consequences of our choices. That does not mean, however, that verbal, physical or emotional abuse is deserved.

No, you didn't "deserve" it. Dressing like she was "asking for it" is garbage thinking.

Bottom line, there is never any reason or justification for assault or abuse. No one ever has a right to harm or take what they want without our permission. This includes what happens within a committed, engaged or marital relationship.

No relationship entitles any man to do anything to any woman. Hear me clearly. Agreed upon sexual relations once is not a free pass forever. "No" means no.

It doesn't matter what has transpired in past relationships. It doesn't matter what has happened in a current relationship. Healthy people let you say no. They respect (and want to know!) your opinions and preferences. Our responsibility is to get in touch with what we think and feel and learn to express it.

Learn that "No" is a complete sentence. [*6]

This quote from *The art of "no."* (captainawkward.com) really sums it up:

*Women are socialized to make men feel good. We're socialized to "let you down easy." We're not socialized to say a clear and direct "no." We're socialized to speak in hints and boost egos and let people save face. People who don't respect the social contract (rapists, predators, assholes, pickup artists) are good at taking advantage of this. "No" is something we have to learn. "No" is something we have to earn. In fact, I'd argue that the ability to just say "no" to something, without further comment, apology, explanation, guilt, or thinking about it is one of the great rites of passage in growing up, and when you start saying it and saying it regularly the world often pushes back. And calls you names.* [*7]

To me, it's ironic and sad, judgement is still initially assigned and assumed on the part of the victim. There is no excuse for abuse.

> "Every time we impose our will on another, it is an act of violence."- Ghandi

# SURRENDER YOUR SHAME

My friend, you've carried the secrets and the shame far too long. It's time to let them go. Congratulations on your courage to make it this far.

We began our journey in the Recognize Your Hurts section. It's time to Release Your Shame.

It's time to take the power away from the hurts.

Part of surrendering and releasing your shame comes as you take back what was taken from you in the first place. Remember, there is a difference between guilt and shame.

Shame is going to affect your personal perception of your worth and value. Imagine taking a beautiful rose bud and wrapping plastic wrap around it. Eventually, it will fade, be no longer recognizable, and certainly it's never fulfilled its full potential.

Living with a scarlet letter or mask is much the same. The hurts suffocate our fullness. Acknowledging and understanding the roots of our shame are crucial first steps in surrendering those feelings and thriving.

*I remember the day I had my heart breakthrough. It was Saturday, April 19, 2008.*

*I was attending a self-development weekend. We had feedback exercises, writing assignments, interactions with small groups, large groups, even one-on-one time. We were bonding and learning to trust. When the challenge of the breakthrough began, I was ready.*

*I had carried one specific burden for a decade. It was an assault I could clearly recall. Each time I did, I felt sickened. Yet, I didn't know who to tell, if I was "justified" in my feelings, and what if anything needed to be done.*

*I engaged in a process designed to make me open the flood gates and let the dam burst. And burst it did. I dealt with that incident and others from years before that I had been harboring and excusing.*

*Once the exercise was complete, I literally felt lighter both in years and poundage. I'd let the baggage, the shame, and the darkness go. For the first time in decades, I felt my whole heart beating. In the past, I had tried to save it from further damage by building walls, wrapping it in barbed wire, even going so far as to erect an invisible titanium barrier around it. I was free.*

*It was the first time in our twenty year marriage I was able to say to my husband, "I love you with my whole heart." Because I finally felt it and could.*

As Brene' Brown shares in her book, Daring Greatly, "Wholehearted living is about engaging in our lives from a place of worthiness. It means cultivating the courage, compassion, and connection to wake up in the morning and think, *No matter what gets done and how much is left undone, I am enough.* It's going to bed at night thinking, *Yes, I am imperfect and vulnerable and sometimes afraid, but that doesn't change the truth that I am also brave and worthy of love and belonging.*"

Without a clear understanding of the difference between guilt and shame, it's easy for guilt to accumulate and manifest itself as shame.

*I clearly recall an incident prior to my heart breakthrough.*

*I had been given verbal permission to use program material from a fellow author. I had paid for, attended, and participated in half a dozen of her workshops in the recent past. When I shared with her that I was adding her resources to my toolbox and giving her full credit, she flipped out; threatening me with a cease and desist order if I didn't take down the content immediately.*

*Initially, I was shocked, stunned even. These feelings led to guilt and eventually to shame. Thankfully, I came to realize, I wasn't wrong and I hadn't done anything wrong. It was simply a misunderstanding.*

*However, because of my past abuse, I thought doing something "wrong" meant I was "wrong."*

Why do I share this? Because I know and understand the slippery slope from guilt to shame.

In Nathaniel Hawthorne's book, The Scarlet Letter, Hester wore her shame for all to see. For a season, it was her identity. However, with time, Hester grew stronger through her trials.

We, too, can release our shame and hold our heads high. Our past does not have to define us. We can allow it to shape us and prepare us to be a voice for ourselves as well as others.

It's time to put your voice to use. It's time to break the stronghold of what's been keeping you bound. It's time to release your shame.

Hold on. Don't shut down or stop now. I promise we'll go slowly and you will have choices.

As an expert and leader in the field of the Shame Resilience Theory, Brene' Brown presents three steps to recognize and pass through shame. Using them, we can move forward and not get stuck resulting in withering and fading like the rosebud I mentioned earlier.

- Talk to yourself like you talk to someone you love. "I would say to myself, 'God, you're so stupid, Brene,'" Brown says. "I would never talk to my kids that way."
- Reach out to someone you trust.
- Tell your story. "Shame cannot survive being spoken," Brown says.[8]

You will need your writings from before and a trusted confidant. Based on your beliefs and experiences, this could be a mental health professional, a member of the clergy, a friend who has proven themselves trustworthy, or perhaps a family member.

Things to consider before you share your shame.

What is the relationship, if any, of the person with whom you're going to share in conjunction to the person or persons you will be sharing about? For example, if you were hurt by an uncle, his spouse (your aunt) or your parent (his sibling), may not be the best person to share your experience with for the first time.

What is the emotional stability and maturity of the person with whom you are going to share?

How have they earned your trust? Trust is not something we need to give freely to each and every one.

Personally, I always pray and ask for my potential confidant to be revealed to me. Maybe your gut has a certain suggestion for you. It may also suggest who not to share with. Heed that prompting.

Once you have made your selection, ask permission to share.

For your safety and respect for your confidant, don't blurt your story out in a public place during an impromptu or casual meeting. These are your deepest wounds that may have been hiding for decades. You want to fully release them without the possibility of re-injury or backlash.

Remember when I talked about verbal abuse and its damaging effects? The tongue can be a double edged sword cutting through our bone and marrow, penetrating our soul.

Let's reframe the image of the tongue and the power of words. Instead of a sword, envision the tongue as a fire.

"So also the tongue is a small thing, but what enormous damage it can do. A great forest can be set on fire by one tiny spark."- James 3:5 (TLB)

One strategy farmers employ in order to enhance the quality of their crop yield is to set fire to their fields. What was once poor producing comes back healthier and stronger.

We can do the same with the lies associated with the hurts of our past causing our unhealthy shame.

Let's set fire to what once was producing poorly in order to yield a healthier, stronger self-image and life!

I'm referring to what I implied back in the healing your hurt section. You'll need the pages, journal, or notebook used to record your hurts. Now, decide on an open area that isn't dry or perhaps a fire pit or fireplace. Also, have a fire source available- matches, lighter, whatever. And oh, yes, we are.

We're going to set fire to those memories. Light them up and let them fade away. As the flames engulf the words and pages, allow the process to create a purification of your soul. Cleanse your heart, mind, and spirit of the feelings, images, and experiences that caused your hurts. Let them drift away in the smoke and the ashes fly away releasing you from the prison of shame that's been holding you captive.

Instead of wrapping our heart in barbed wire, sealing it off behind a wall or shielding it with plastic wrap in an attempted act of protection and from possible further harm, we can lovingly and gently embrace it. Our heart will come alive. We take on a new rhythm. Just like Irene Cara sang, "Oh, what a feeling!"

## References for Strength and Release

"And you will know the truth, and the truth will set you free."- John 8:32 NLT

Time doesn't heal all wounds; forgiveness does.

"Come now, let's settle this," says the Lord. "Though your sins are like scarlet, I will make them as white as snow. Though they are red like crimson, I will make them as white as wool."- Isaiah 1:18 (NLT)

No, dear brothers and sisters, I have not achieved it,[a] but I focus on this one thing: Forgetting the past and looking forward to what lies ahead, I press on to reach the end of the race and receive the heavenly prize for which God, through Christ Jesus, is calling us.- Philippians 3:13-15 (NLT)

Don't judge yourself by your past. You don't live there anymore.

"Fear not, for you will not be put to shame; and do not feel humiliated, for you will not be disgraced; but you will forget the shame of your youth, and the reproach of your widow-hood you will remember no more. For your husband is your Maker, Whose name is the Lord of hosts; and your Redeemer is the Holy One of Israel, Who is called the God of all the earth. For the Lord has called you, like a wife forsaken and grieved in spirit, even like a wife of one's youth when she is rejected," says your God."- Isaiah 54:4-6 (NASB)

To all who mourn in Israel, He will give a crown of beauty for ashes, a joyous blessing instead of mourning, festive praise instead of despair. In their righteousness, they will be like great oaks that the Lord has planted for His own glory.- Isaiah 61:3 (NLT)

"A moment of self-compassion can change your entire day. A string of such moments can change the course of your life." —Christopher K. Germer

"The past has no power over the present moment." —Eckhart Tolle

"Lack of forgiveness causes almost all of our self-sabotaging behavior." —Mark Victor Hansen

"Forgiveness is giving up the hope that the past could be any different." —Oprah Winfrey

Bitterness is poisoning ourselves while wishing harm on another.

"Only if you've been in the deepest valley can you ever know how magnificent it is to be on the highest mountain." —Richard Nixon

# RECLAIM YOUR VOICE

*"Anxiety thrives in the darkness of denial.*
*But when we face anxiety in the light of truth it runs."*
*– An Imperfect Woman*

# IT'S OKAY TO TELL "SECRETS"

"Promise not to tell?" It can be perceived as privileged insider information or a bit of intimacy and bonding.

It can also be a threat, in case you do consider telling. "You better not tell. This is a secret."

There is a stark difference between a secret and a surprise.

*One of my dad's favorite stories about me as a young child is a great example of the difference between the two.*

*I think I was five years old at the time and it was his birthday. His gift from me was going to be a new belt. I knew he'd be very excited. "He cleaned up good," as the expression goes. My daddy loved to dress nice.*

*Another thing he loved was to tease me. I remember the first time he told me I had epidermis all over me. He told me I was covered in it. Thankfully, my mom begged him to explain when she saw my panicked reaction.*

*He was clever and could always manage a way to catch me off guard. The fact that he was a police officer, professionally trained and highly experienced with interrogation skills, made it hard for me to outsmart him.*

*This particular year, he was ready to give me a hard time as he tried to pry a hint out of me about his gift. I was ready for him, though. He pressed and I would not budge. He asked and I evaded. Finally, feeling like a victorious warrior having survived the inquisition, I smugly declared, "I'm not even going to tell you what color belt I got you for your birthday." Yeah, that didn't go as I planned.*

While to me it's a sweet fond memory, it also serves as a clear example. A surprise is something that makes someone else feel good. It's a blessing or treat for them. Special things meant to be revealed and released at just the right time. A proposal, a sonogram result, an unexpected visit from a loved one. These are all great examples of surprises.

A secret on the other hand may be something that needs to be shared. "You're not going to tell anyone are you?" "Shhhh, don't you dare tell anyone or I'll _____." If a threat is issued or tied to the words, telling is exactly what needs to happen.

While at the time I felt as though I had shared a secret, the worst offense I committed was revealing a surprise before its time. The secrets associated with hurts are intended to remain in the dark and as long as they do, they have power over us.

It's time to reclaim your voice. To get your power back; power you may have lost at such a young age you weren't even aware you possessed it.

# SHATTER THE STRONGHOLD

A common expression in the world of recovery is, "We're only as sick as our secrets." Once the light has been shed, what's in the dark no longer has the power to control us.

Tony Robbins says, "Your past does not equal your future." We can break free and break the assumed mold.

In the last section, I shared the first time I verbalized my traumas. For decades, I both justified and compared my past to other peoples'. Since the majority of my hurts were single incidents, I wondered if they "counted." I measured my hurts and pain to the stories I read about in magazines or heard about on the news. Because none of mine were "that bad," I wound up minimizing my hurts and shame.

I was able to reason or excuse a large majority of my assaults. However, if they weren't such a "big deal" why did I keep them a secret?

The prison of silence. While the bars are open wide enough to pass a hand through, they are narrow enough to keep us trapped.

As long as we allow silence, the assault and the assaulter, the hurt and the happening, they hold the power. Once the first word is uttered; yes the first time it's spoken out loud, the stronghold is shattered!

Hiding the secrets impacts the way we see ourselves and the value we place on ourselves.

Part of the good news and some of our hope can be found when we realize we have a choice. We can either be a silent sufferer or a spoken survivor.

The journey of being a survivor begins when we separate facts from feelings. The declaration of survivor can be the first step of release from unhealthy shame. We no longer define ourselves by the actions that took place.

In my mind, if I didn't talk about it, maybe it hadn't happened. Maybe it wasn't really *that* bad. If I didn't breathe life into it by talking about it, maybe it wouldn't have power over me. In reality, the more I kept quiet, the longer I tried to numb and ignore the pain, the stronger its effect was on me.

Silence can be a powerful tool. It can represent anger or acceptance. In my case, I grew weary of wearing a mask and pretending everything was okay, that I had not been affected by others' choices. I began to accept my past as a definition of my identity.

*I recall another incident in high school, and with another popular jock from a different high school, was the first time*

*I ever stopped anything before it went too far. "Rod" was dreamy, the epitome of a Texas linebacker, strong and solid. He paid attention to ME, the girl who felt insignificant and discarded.*

*During a get together at his house at which his parents were absent (and, yes, there was underage drinking), we snuck off to his bedroom. The two of us started talking a little which led to kissing a little. Then he decided to make his move.*

*He asked me to perform a certain act on him. I said no. He pressed, asking again. He even went so far as to pressure me with the fact I had led him on. After all, I went back to his room.*

*That was the first time I remember ever standing up for myself. I flat out refused to do what he wanted and I didn't.*

*You guessed it, we wound up not going out after that. I'm pretty sure we wouldn't have anyway. Sure, I may have lost out on dinner and a movie, even being known because of who I was dating; however, I was able to keep some pride and self-worth. I was able to experience for a moment, the power of valuing myself.*

It only takes one time, one step to stop or break the cycle. If or when a next time happens, we've already got one victory to rely on and call upon. Once can be enough, if we build on it.

# TAKE BACK WHAT
# WAS TAKEN

Once we have been hurt and held prisoner by strong-holds, we are not able to reclaim our innocence. Once taken, it cannot be wholly returned. We can, however, claim and own our value.

Internal dialog or talking to ourselves begins around age 3.

Based on the age you were when your hurts began to take place, it may be challenging to now start speaking to yourself in a kinder, healthier manner.

Once we have shattered the lies we believed about our worth, those things that keep us suffering in silence, our voice can begin to re-emerge.

**Tiffany** found healing and restoration for her marriage through a series of steps over time. Much of it came during her quiet time with God.

Often, we have to be quiet in order to hear the truth from that still small voice within.

Tiffany had scars that only the Ultimate Healer could repair. Through prayer, reading the Word of God, believing God, and applying it consistently to her life, she began to see a change both in her heart and in her marriage. She often journaled her hurts and emotions, and she allowed God to speak to her heart and bring healing one step at a time.

As a result, Tiffany was able to put the past behind her permanently. She learned to love herself and forgive those who violated her. She put the past where it belonged - in the past.

**Kirsten** shares her journey in reclaiming her voice. "Praise God, He redeems the brokenhearted. As I continue to work through the hurt, I'm learning to lean into Jesus daily. Each day is a choice to walk with Jesus, to trust Him, to trust Dave [her husband], to be authentic in my relationships with Dave and others, and to believe God is crazy about me. I'm learning my seat at God's table isn't in the corner, picking up crumbs. Instead, I sit with the Trinity, enjoy fellowship with them, and converse with them, confident that I am fully known and eternally loved."

If Kirsten could speak with you, she would say:

"First of all, I'm sorry for your hurt. You are wounded. Your pain is real and legitimate.

"Second, you are not alone. God the Father is near.

"Third, God has provided a way out through your pain. Trust Him to walk with you every step of the way.

"Fourth, find some trusted friends who will pray for you and with you. Find your 'Jesus with skin on' people.

"Fifth, your past *describes* you but it doesn't have to *define* you."

**Jeanna** encourages, "Healing comes upon request. The journey is where healing is found. It is not a destination station. Always be ready."

**Erica** recalls, "As I battled all those emotions, God began to teach me the difference between sympathy and compassion. He showed me that sympathy is feeling sorry for the person, pitying them from a distance, causing the person to remain in their victimized state. Compassion is when you walk alongside someone. It is when you see greatness in them and you help to propel them out of their victim mentality. Jesus was moved with compassion all throughout the New Testament, which caused people to be changed forever."

**Dalia** replaced her lies with truth, The Truth. The only One who could fully satisfy her was God. Instead of pursuing a man, she began to pursue The One who has and will always treasure her. Her true healing, peace, and restoration comes from her vertical alignment.

**Lisa** realized she could let her "stuff" rule her or she could rule over her "stuff." also known as lies. Her personal development through her spiritual development gave her the strength to replace her "stuff" or lies with truth. Her healing helped produce in her a capacity to serve others. She recognizes God doesn't give us anything we can't handle and, with and through Him, we can handle anything.

**Debra** discovered four steps she could apply to the smallest disappointment or the greatest tragedy. We can and are forgiven when we allow ourselves to be washed clean and accept the freedom that accompanies it. "The encouragements I would give anyone who has had an abortion are- abortion is not the unforgivable sin. Your baby is fine and in the presence of Jesus and many people who love it. Through Jesus you have the hope of holding and being with that child again. Until then, you can live a full life. The enemy comes to steal, kill and destroy but Jesus died that we could live an abundant life. The scriptures did not say, we could live an abundant life as long as we don't screw it up too bad."

You may have begun to notice that throughout this entire book, action is the initial step to healing. Each woman who has shared part of her story, decided to change. Decide comes from two Latin words. De meaning off and caedere meaning cut. We decided to "cut off" the power of the lies.

We recognized our hurts. We released our shame. We reclaimed our voice.

We made the choice to DIG Deep, as Brene Brown observes in her book, *The Gifts of Imperfection*. DIG stands for:

Deliberate in their thoughts and behaviors throughout prayer, meditation, or simply setting the intention.

Inspired to make new and different choices.

Going. They take action.

You can as well. You are capable.

"You is kind. You is smart. You is important."- from Dreamworks, The Help.

# VICTORY IN YOUR VOICE

It's time to start telling yourself new information. It's time to live in truth. Your voice and your peace go hand-in-hand. There's an expression I've heard for years. "What you think about you bring about." It's time to see yourself in a new way, as you are new each day.

Whether someone believes in law-of-attraction mantras, Biblical truth, or positive affirmations, what we program in our mind determines the way we see ourselves. The way we see ourselves determines the way we treat ourselves. The way we treat ourselves lets other people know how we expect to be treated as well.

No billboard needs to be rented nor a mountaintop proclamation be heralded. This is an inside job.

Speaking the words for the first time will seem awkward and clumsy, a bit like a toddlers first steps. However, when we do so, we unleash a new power. It breaks the silence of shame.

Giving voice to the truth is a beautiful sound in the process of letting go.

It may need to begin in the quiet of a darkened room with no one else there, whispered to yourself and barely audible. As you grow stronger, you'll be able to say it louder and louder until you could shout it from the mountaintop or rent a billboard of proclamation.

As hard as this has been up until now - your healing, your future - YOU are so worth it!

Reclaiming your voice is empowering, exciting, energizing.

When we begin to speak truth, we crush the lies and soften the betrayals. We add a soothing salve to the wounds that have been open, possibly hidden, for oh so long. We literally have the opportunity to speak life and truth into what was once dead and damaged.

We're going to create a new self-image. It's been said the most important voice we ever hear is our own. Assuming that truth, let's begin talking to ourselves in a new way. It's time to reprogram those nasty negative messages and tapes.

"God, please help me see myself the way You see me and help me to forgive myself and to receive Your unmerited grace. I desperately need You to teach me how to love myself as a divorced person. I need to embrace Your love for me. Help me to see that Your love will cast out all my fear and anger and any title that I am now given."- Erica McCuen

Imagine holding a newborn child. Pause for a moment. Really picture that newborn, the color of the blanket that swaddles him or her, rays of sun casting a glow atop that little bald head. Take in a deep breath. Can you imagine that "new baby smell?"

Now, what words would you speak over that child?

What terms of endearment, empowerment, and blessing would you utter?

Now say those same words to yourself. They may be merely a whisper at first. They may feel uncomfortable, like a new pair of shoes you've been admiring perhaps even noticed someone else wearing. You finally get the courage to try them on and aren't confident they'll fit. It may take a bit of stretching to feel comfortable in them. Yet, you want them so badly, you're willing to break them in, slowly.

Let those words wash over you and soak in.

How do you feel?

Do you feel honored? Valued? Respected? Appreciated?

Now look directly into a mirror and stare into your soul through your eyes. Don't be distracted by facial features, makeup or lack thereof. It doesn't matter if you're having a good or bad hair day. The gift of your worth and value are priceless regardless of the wrapping. We are concentrating on internal assets.

Those very words you would speak to a little unharmed innocent child are the same words we need to say to ourselves.

Writing them will be as or even more powerful. So let's do that next.

Here are a few of the things I say to myself as an example:

"I am a worthy and respected woman allowing God to work through me as I lead and encourage women to allow their hearts to heal and love themselves as Christ does."

"I can and have let go of my past. It describes what happened to me. It no longer defines me."

"I love my strength, my determination, my resilience."

Now it's your turn.

I am _____

I can _____

I love my _____

Once you've reclaimed your voice, promise yourself you'll never let it be taken from you again.

## References for Strength and Release

Personalize these scriptures. Make them about YOU!

Here's an example. Psalm 91:14-16 (NIV) is read:

"Because he loves me," says the Lord, "I will rescue him; I will protect him, for he acknowledges my name. He will call upon me, and I will answer him; I will be with him in trouble, I will deliver him and honor him. With long life I will satisfy him and show him my salvation."

OR when customized, "Because Daphne loves me," says the Lord, "I will rescue her. I will protect Daphne for she acknowledges my name. Daphne will call upon me, and I will answer her; I will be with her in trouble, I will deliver her and honor her. With long life will I satisfy Daphne and show her my salvation."

This means that anyone who belongs to Christ has become a new person. The old life is gone; a new life has begun! - 2 Corinthians 5:17 (NLT)

"I will give you back your health again and heal your wounds."- Jeremiah 30:17 (TLB)

"I am sure that God who began the good work within you will keep right on helping you grow in his grace until His task within you is finally finished on the day when Jesus Christ returns."- Philippians 1:6 (TLB)

"Don't let the noise of others' opinions drown out your own inner voice"- Steve Jobs

"I now free myself from destructive fears and doubts."- Louise Hay

No one can take away the power I have within me.

I have a right to be free from abuse. Every human being has that right and I do, too.

I never give up; I keep going.

I love myself unconditionally just as I am.

"Faith is the only thing I know of that is stronger than fear."- Joyce Meyer

# FINAL THOUGHTS

Before we say farewell.........

Throughout all of my experiences, one thing has been my anchor and salvation. Hope.

I've known all along, after and sometimes during every instance, there was something better for my future. I held onto a peace that comes through faith.

Maybe you're familiar with the saying, "In life, things that happen to us can make us better or bitter." Or, since by now you know I relate a lot of life to songs, "What doesn't kill you makes you stronger."

I never wanted to cave, give into or believe the lies, the hurts, and betrayals.

More than twenty five years ago, I was introduced to someone for whom I am eternally grateful and I consider a true angel.

Her name was Pam Jones. We lived across the country from one another. It was through a series of other relationships that we connected. The point of introduction came when she flew to Dallas for cancer treatments and I got to be her driver to the appointments.

I got to know a woman who was fighting for her life. A wife, mother of two, and one who was still working for the postal service while selling Mary Kay on the side. In it all, she had a peace about her that was undeniable. It literally shone from within.

On one of the drives to and from the airport and oncologist, I summoned the courage to ask. I had to know more about her source. How could she, in light of all that she was facing, still have hope and peace?

That was when she shared her faith with me. Up to that point, my faith had really been based more on "religion," rules instead of relationship. Thanks to Pam's openness and literally dying desire to love and serve others, I accepted Jesus Christ as my Lord and Savior.

I have no way of knowing where you are in your faith, my fellow traveler of life and now sister in the scarlet letter. I will not presume nor try to pressure. I simply invite you. If you have not accepted the forgiveness and grace that comes through accepting Jesus, I invite you to do so. Your sins and shame can be erased and healed.

If you've not been able to find hope, here is a great first step and place to start.

It doesn't have to be a public display or an official ceremony. You can go to Him exactly as you are, where you are, right in this very moment. I assure you, you will be lovingly welcomed and accepted.

Your first step is to **admit**.

> Admit you've tried to live life on your own terms, seeking approval and acceptance from others while carrying the weight of sin, shame and regret. Admit you're ready for a change.

Now, **believe**.

> Believe you can be forgiven. Believe and accept unconditional love from someone you've never met, yet who knew you before you were born; someone who was willing to give their life for you. Yes, this may be a big stretch of your ability to imagine and believe, but simply try. Release the darkness and lies you've held onto for so long.

Finally, **commit**.

> Commit to a new way of life and living. Commit to turning from your now former ways of thinking and accepting your past as your definition of worth. Commit to embracing a fresh approach in how you see yourself, love yourself, and forgive those who've hurt you in the past.

"Dear Lord Jesus, I know that I am a sinner, and I ask for Your forgiveness. I believe You died for my sins and rose from the dead. I turn from my sins and invite You to come into my heart and life. I want to trust and follow You as my Lord and Savior. In Your Name. Amen"- Billy Graham

If you chose to accept this hope, a huge step in healing and forgiveness, congratulations and welcome to a forever family. We're not perfect. We're simply promised.

But what if you don't "feel" any different right away? Give it time. Like a seed planted in fresh soil, with time and nurturing something beautiful will grow.

My simple desire for you is a better day tomorrow than today. As we heal from our past, as the scarlet letters are erased and the masks are shattered, a new light shines in us and through us.

It takes courage to recognize your hurts. It takes strength to release your shame. It takes bravery to reclaim your voice.

Well done good and faithful one, well done.

No more days wasting away
I finally realized the gift inside of me

Dara Maclean…..Free

# APPENDIX

*1- http://healthywa.wa.gov.au/Articles/A_E/
About-sexual-assault

*2 https://www.healthyplace.com/
abuse/emotional-psychological-abuse/
emotional-abuse-definitions-signs-symptoms-examples/

*3 http://www.survivingtherapistabuse.
com/2015/12/article-30-signs-of-emotional-abus
e-in-a-relationship/

*4 http://outofthefog.website/
top-100-trait-blog/2015/11/4/grooming

*5 http://outofthefog.website/
top-100-trait-blog/2015/11/4/grooming

*6 https://drkathleenyoung.
wordpress.com/2012/06/25/
how-to-avoid-an-abuser-understanding-grooming/

*7 https://drkathleenyoung.
wordpress.com/2012/06/25/
how-to-avoid-an-abuser-understanding-grooming/

*8 https://www.huffingtonpost.com/2013/10/08/
brene-brown-shame-oprah_n_4059675.html

# ADDITIONAL RESOURCES

If you have young children and seek resources for a deeper understanding of their development, visit https://www.gracepointwellness.org

More information on grooming can be found here: https://abuseandrelationships.org/Content/Behaviors/grooming.html

http://victimsofcrime.org/media/reporting-on-child-sexual-abuse/grooming-dynamic-of-csa

Signs of emotional abuse: https://www.psychologytoday.com/blog/toxic-relationships/201704/forms-emotional-and-verbal-abuse-you-may-be-overlooking

Covert or Passive Aggressive Behavior:
https://www.liveabout.com/
passive-aggressive-behavior-a-form-o
f-covert-abuse-1102402

Dr Darv Smith
http://www.darvsmith.com

# SUGGESTED BOOKS FOR FURTHER INFORMATION AND INCREASED AWARENESS

Woman Thou Art Loosed!- T.D. Jakes

Daring Greatly- Brene' Brown, Ph.D, L.M.S.W.

The Gift of Imperfection- Brene' Brown, Ph.D, L.M.S.W.

Your Secret Name- Kary Oberbrunner

# ABOUT THE AUTHOR

Daphne V Smith has a heart for the hurting. She herself lived for years in silence and shame as the result of decades of abuse. With the loving support and encouragement of her husband David, she sought truth and healing. Thanks to a new awareness, a desire to live by example, and commitment to serving her Creator, Daphne found her voice and nothing will ever again silence her.

She began her writing career as a contributor to several books on Christian living, a Bible study, retreat curriculum, as well as blogging. Daphne has an insatiable appetite for learning which leads to new levels of healing and opportunity for herself and in order to encourage others.

Daphne associates with others in pursuit of excellence and personal development. Her success in direct sales as a three-time car winner and passion for encouraging entrepreneurs fuels her creativity and produces results.

Daphne has spoken at retreats and conferences across the country and has been behind more than one pulpit. Involved with BNI, a requested emcee, certified by the Cooper Institute for Aerobics and Research, American Association of Christian Counselors, and the John Maxwell Team, she loves to customize her message to her audience in order to best serve their needs.

If you were to sit down for a cup of coffee or adult beverage, one of the first things Daphne would ask you is, "How is it with your soul?"

She believes in living life by design instead of default or, as Daphne refers to it, living a Well Done Life. There's no need to live another day behind the façade. You deserve to experience freedom and to move forward with and on purpose.

Connect at: DaphneVSmith.com

# ACKNOWLEDGEMENTS

*To my husband David. Thank you for healing along with me, for your unwavering support and belief in my ability to write this book. I look forward to my next book, our first together.*

*To our son Connor, thank you. You've taught to embrace my creativity and challenged me to expand my understanding of myself and others. I love you Boo and am proud of you.*

*To our daughter-in-love Alexis. God has a plan for our family and I am blessed it includes you. Your strength, courage, and sense of adventure inspire me.*

*To all of my family, thank you for your love and unconditional acceptance of me just as I have been, am, and who I will become. I am stronger because of you.*

*To my chosen "sisters." Your belief, your example, your occasional kick in the rump were my stepping stones and anchor. If this resonates with you, you're one of them.*

*Florence Chapman Littauer, Betty Southard, Marita Littauer Tedder, Georgia Shaffer, Linda Jewel - thank you for leading the way and planting seeds before me and within me. Your successes encouraged me to press on.*

*To my home girls - we've shared the blood and the mud. Thank you for loving and supporting me all the way through. Especially to you, Joyce, thank you for going first. I no longer think you're crazy. This was tough and worth it. To God be the glory!*

*Jeanna Scott - your willingness to serve and share is inspiring. Thank you for always desiring more growth.*

*To Kary Oberbrunner, David Branderhorst and every member of the Igniting Souls Tribe, thank you for your encouragement. Your desire to achieve your dreams has been fuel to my fire.*

*Brad Franklin, MAMFT, LPC- thank you for teaching me that subjecting myself to abuse is not a way to honor God; and for introducing me to a program that allowed me to get my heart back. It was one of the most pivotal events in my recovery.*

*(posthumously) Dell Christy Tyson, RN, MA, LPC, LMFT - Thank you for living, loving, and leading by example. It's okay to be a strong woman clear in my boundaries, allowing myself to experience my feelings all while being a Christian.*

# ADDITIONAL OPPORTUNITIES FOR CONNECTION

**Erica Foster**- Author of You Taught My Feet To Dance: Learning to Follow His Lead

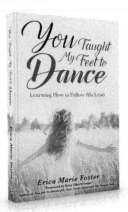

You can reach Erica through:
**Website:** www.EricaMarieFoster.com

---

**Dalia Franco**- Author of One Proposal: A 60-Day Devotional While Waiting On The One To Marry

You can find Dalia on:
**Instagram:** @daliamfranco
**Webiste:** www.DaliaFranco.com

**Tiffany Godfrey**- Author of Christian Marriage Coaching in a Box: How a Wife Can Heal From Insecurity And Mend a Broken Marriage (The Wife Coach Series) (Volume 1)

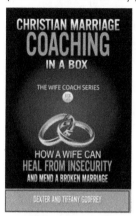

Connect with Tiffany through:
**Website:** www.CommittedWife.com
**LinkedIn:** https://www.linkedin.com/in/relationshipmissionaries
**Facebook:** http://www.facebook.com/RelationshipMissionaries
**Instagram:** https://www.instagram.com/relationship_missionaries
**Twitter:** https://twitter.com/relationship757
**Pinterest:** http://www.pinterest.com/CommittedWife

---

**Debra Hayes**- Author of RISE: What to Do When Hell Won't Back Off

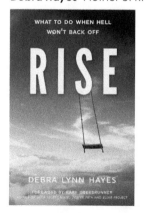

Reach Debra by:
**Website:** www.DebraLynnHayes.com
**Email:** debra@DebraLynnHayes.com

**Lisa Moser**- Author of, Miss Conception: 5 Steps to Overcome Our Misconceptions and Achieve Our Own Crowning Moments

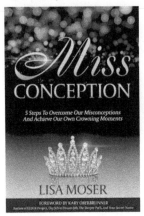

Meet Lisa at:
**Website:** http://www.LisaMoser.com
**Facebook:** https://www.facebook.com/LisaMoserLive/
**Instagram:** @LisaMoserLive

---

**Kirsten Samuel**- Author of Choosing a Way Out: When the Bottom Isn't the Bottom

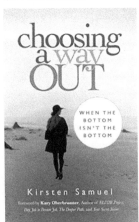

Connect with Kirsten through:
**Website:** www.KirstenDSamuel.com

# BRING DAPHNE INTO
## your business or organization

**Author. Speaker. Retreat Facilitator.**

Daphne knows the importance of choosing a speaker to meet your needs. The right one sets the tone and engages the audience for success. Daphne's authentic approach, digestible content, and high energy qualifies her as a top choice for conferences, non-profits, and small group events. She customizes each message and focuses on your group's objectives.

## Contact Daphne today to begin the conversation DaphneVSmith.com

CPSIA information can be obtained
at www.ICGtesting.com
Printed in the USA
BVHW04s2105130918
527458BV00015B/52/P